Lyric Voices

Lyric Voices
APPROACHES TO THE POETRY
OF CONTEMPORARY SONG

Barbara Farris Graves
Donald J. McBain

JOHN WILEY & SONS, INC.

New York • London • Sydney • Toronto

Library of Congress Catalogue Card Number: 77-165947

ISBN 0-471-32260-1

Printed in the United States of America.

10 9 8 7 6 5 4 3 2 1

For Christine and Mark

Preface

This book is first and foremost a poetry text. For nearly three centuries following the Renaissance—a period that many scholars have regarded as the last great surge of poetry intended for singing— literary poetry and songs traveled their separate ways. By mid- twentieth century it seemed that the study of songs was destined to be the province of the folklorist cataloging the fading remnants of a once-widespread creative force. Then the phenomenon of rock burst forth. It was perhaps crude and unpoetic in its infancy, but as the six- ties progressed, lyrics of increasing sophistication and skill appeared. Once more, the lyric voice is flowering. The great creative energy of man's stubborn attempt to penetrate the meaning of his existence is surging forth in voices from the streets, voices that weave the sounds of the present with the age-old questions of man in relation to his loved one, his society, and the cosmos.

The vitality of the new lyric poetry has carried it from the streets into the literary world, and in classrooms the lyrics of pop artists are discussed along with the verses of traditional poets. The recent boom in anthologies of song lyrics indicates the song's newly reattained poetic status. Instead of merely presenting another anthol- ogy, however, we wanted to confront the new lyric phenomenon, hoping to put it in some kind of a poetic and cultural perspective. Consequently the book is designed (1) to provide a certain amount of guiding background information, (2) to ask questions that will help the reader probe and make his own conclusions about historical, aesthetic, and cultural aspects of the new lyric poetry, and (3) to offer insights into the nature of poetry in general. It is designed to furnish material that will encourage the reader to venture as far into the subject as he wants and is able to go. Hence the structure can be explained as follows.

The introductory chapter examines the term "lyric" and its changing definition. In addition, the chapter provides background information and attempts to place the anthologized songs in a poetic tradition. As the title—Electric Orphic Circuit—suggests, the first chapter traces an evolutionary cycle of poetry from its origins to the here and now sounds. It offers a thesis that the reader may accept, qualify, or reject; but any choice will require further thought and research.

The heart of the book is, of course, the lyrics themselves. The selections represent what we consider to be the best lyrics of the new movement. All have been written in English in the past decade or so. We have tried to provide a cross section of styles and artists, not really a difficult task, since pop songs now cut across and sometimes blend the previously more separated rock, folk, blues, and country styles.

The actual lyrics comprise three chapters divided so as to group general themes that are both contemporary and universal to poetic expression. The works in Chapter II deal with man either alone or in relation to another. Hence, statements of alienation and of inter-personal love stand side by side on the printed pages. The selections in Chapter III deal with man in relation to his community. Various lyrics take up the nature of community in its various forms. Many are steeped in pessimism; some attempt to find solutions to social problems. But generally and collectively, they decry such social destroyers as war, greed, prejudice, and hate, and they reaffirm the need to build toward that mythical better world. The lyrics in Chapter IV deal with man in direct relation to his universe. Nature, religion, freedom, consciousness, mysticism—many serious concerns are interwoven through the imagery of the songs.

Admittedly, the categories sometimes overlap, and it can be argued of almost any particular work that it could have been placed in another section. We recognize that all attempts at categorization are necessarily arbitrary, and we have more or less let each lyric find its own section by what we believed to be its own internal emphasis. The order of the three sections follows the ideally expanding order of man's awareness—from the strictly personal, to the interpersonal, to the communal, to the universal.

We have included study questions for most of the selections. The aim of these questions is to help broaden and deepen the experience of the song by examining the aesthetics of its form, and by relating it to traditional linear poetry, as well as to other media and events. The questions, however, make no attempt to be all-inclusive. Our primary focus is on poetry, and we have often pur-posely omitted discussing topical issues. Since the songs themselves raise these issues, opportunities will arise for the sociologically-inclined to pursue these matters. We have tried, through the questions, to encourage many varied approaches to getting inside the work. Some questions are standard and traditional; others are unorthodox, but we feel they are worthwhile if they work for the individual—there is more than one way to skin a poem. For some lyrics the list of questions is long and comprehensive. For a few, at the end of each section, we have supplied no questions at all, thereby leaving our readers to devise their own ways of getting into the song . . . and back out again.

Chapter V, "Discussions on Poetic Meaning," is meant to be an inductive presentation of levels and ways in which poems communi-cate meaning. The discussion topics proceed from the poem's literal statement, through image and metaphor, to deeper levels of symbol, myth, and archetype. Critics and academics for so long have directed our attention to the more esoteric forms of poetry, so that they may help us understand it. As a result, the lyric has been largely ignored, especially the modern lyric. Although we have drawn examples as much from traditional linear poetry as from the modern lyric form, the discussions and questions in Chapter V attempt to show that the lyric (and especially the modern lyric, because it can be as esoteric as any other poem) can take its audience on the full journey, from literal statement to archetype.

We have included a reading list and a discography to help those who might want to enrich their knowledge in this area. Needless to say, this lyric movement is brand new, and much work remains to be done.

This text may be used in several ways—for an introductory poetry course, an up-to-date contemporary poetry course, an inter-disciplinary seminar on the lyric, or, simply, as a supplementary reader for a freshman composition course. Some may prefer to start immediately with the lyrics themselves, others with Chapter V; the book is designed to be flexible enough to allow for a rerouting through its pages. We recommend wherever possible that the songs be heard as well as read. Recordings and tapes are readily available, and if funds are not, perhaps individual class members already have recordings of many of the songs. This is one area in which the teacher will definitely learn from his students.

Some confusion may exist as to whether the selections should be termed songs or poems. We believe they are both. To avoid confusion, however, we refer to them as poems when we are discussing the printed or spoken word. We use the term "song" in reference to the total experience of the work, which would, of course, include performance by a singer. Actually, the texts of these works are in many ways merely blueprints, since without speech there is no poem, and without singing there is no song. The authors of these selections are speakers and singers, and poets. We are proud to have the opportunity to discuss their art with you.

Barbara Farris Graves
Donald J. McBain

Contents

CHAPTER ONE

ELECTRIC ORPHIC CIRCUIT

Don't listen to evil rumors; poetry is alive and well. While it is true that the era of T. S. Eliot, Ezra Pound, and Wallace Stevens is over, and that some poets (and critics) are floundering in the wake of these giants, nevertheless more poetry is being written, read, spoken, sung, listened to, and generally appreciated today than perhaps at any time before. And more *kinds* of poetry. A reader looking for recently published poetry can step inside a bookstore and find anything from the word and picture games of John Lennon to the sprawling cosmic chants of Allen Ginsberg to the soft, semiconfessional sonnets of Robert Lowell. Indeed, the post-World War II period has witnessed a parade of variously ephemeral poetic forms, styles, cliques, schools, and movements. Some of these have been highly innovative; some have returned to or developed past traditions. It is difficult to determine whether any have forged new major directions.

In the past decade, forces have gathered to generate a movement whose poets are united often by life style and personal philosophy but principally by the form in which they create—songs, the lyric form. As precursor, prophet, central figure, and sage, Bob Dylan has managed so far to span the movement; at least he saw it through its incipient period, the decade of the sixties. Certainly, he was the first popular songwriter in quite some time to be considered as a poet, although his right to this title has been battered back and forth by all the people who enjoy that sort of thing. People whose poetic backgrounds range from amateur to aesthete have reacted to the phenomenon that Dylan helped to set in motion and that his verse represents. Some have demeaned it for its illiteracy. Some have said that he is only a songwriter and not a poet, and that his art form is outside the realm of modern poetry. Others have proclaimed him the first poet laureate of mass media. Such divergent critical reactions, however, sometimes indicate more about the particular commentators or about the cultural divergences in our society than they do about either Dylan's verse or the movement.

Nevertheless, the movement has made inroads, even in academic circles. Significantly, the high schools were the first to teach current songs in English classes, though usually smuggled into the course by either a hip or a desperate teacher rather than as part of the regular curriculum. More recently, college poetry courses and texts have been including song lyrics, and some schools have offered seminars in "rock" poetry. This must mean the movement has arrived. The questions arise, though: Will it be a major direction? Is it new? Poet Allen Ginsberg, himself not completely accepted in the more high-brow academic strata, in a recent anthology called *Naked Poetry*, offered a key to the phenomenon:

". . . But young minstrels have now arisen on the airwaves whose poetic forms outwardly resemble antique verse including regular stanzas refrains and rhymes: Dylan and Donovan and some fragments of the Rolling Stones because they *think* not only in words but also in music simultaneously have out of the necessities of their own space-age media and electric machinery tunes evolved a natural use of—a personal realistic imaginative rhymed verse. Principle of composition here is, however, unlike antique literary form, primarily spontaneous and improvised (in the studio if need be at the last minute) and prophetic in character in that tune and language are invoked shamanistically on the spot from the unconscious. The new ear is not dead only for eye-page, it's connected with a voice improvising, with hesitancies aloud, a living musician's ear. The old library poets had lost their voices; natural voice was rediscovered, and now natural song for physical voice. Oddly, this fits Pound's paradigm tracing the degeneration of Poesy from the Greek dance-foot-chorus thru minstrel song thru 1900 abstract voiceless page. So now returned to song and song forms we may yet anticipate inspired Creators like Shiva Krishna Chaitanya. . . ."

Allen Ginsberg, "Some Metamorphoses of Personal Prosody," in *Naked Poetry: Recent American Poetry in Open Forms*, ed. Stephen Berg and Robert Mezey (New York: Bobbs-Merrill Co., Inc., 1969), p. 221.

"Returned to song and song forms": Ginsberg's words suggest a kind of cyclical pattern, one whose first "revolution" is just now being achieved. It is worthwhile to investigate this idea as an introduction to this book. Hopefully, our investigation will enable us to put these anthologized songs in a historical perspective that dates further back than the rockabilly days of Bill Haley and his Comets, and to establish inroads for further study in this area. In considering an evolutionary cycle of poetry, and specifically lyric poetry, there are four periods that demand our attention—the origins of poetry, the Greek lyric, the Renaissance, and the modern electric lyric. Although evolution is a continuous process, these are recognizable stages and focal points of the development of poetry as it meets us today.

The arts of poetry and music had a common origin in primitive song, in what the Greeks were later to call "lyric." These early songs probably consisted of many different kinds—work songs, love songs, lullabies, laments. Song, however, is essentially a public art. Historians, anthropologists, and linguists continue to speculate on the specific date and form of the first actual lyric. However, it is generally agreed on and sustained by the earliest findings of lyric poetry that the lyric grew out of ritualistic patterns surrounding primitive religious ceremonies, and was usually an expression of some kind of mystical experience that the poet was undergoing.

Certain key characteristics, then, should be noted concerning what can be considered the genesis of our poetry. The first is that words and music were conceived as a fused unit, evolving perhaps from spontaneous cries around the ceremonial fires, to chants, and eventually to the story-lyric or ballad. The poet, throughout this development, thought "not only in words but in music simultaneously." Second, since the poet was originally associated with mysticism and magic, poetry was rooted in the realm of the supernatural and the divine. Third, the emphasis was on performance; many of the songs were improvised "shamanistically on the spot from the unconscious." Finally, the entire group participated in the performance, echoing and answering the single voice (this function developed into the Greek "chorus" and, in our modern lyrical poetry, we see its remnant in the refrain, an atrophied, surrogate form of audience participation). Hence the beginnings, and perhaps the essence of poetry, can be found in the primitive lyric, a form that was intense, spontaneous, visceral, communal, magical, mystical . . . and music.

In the Greek period the lyric grew in number and complexity, developing into a profusion of types, such as the triumph, the dirge, the dance-song, the hymn, the processional, and culminating in the fully developed ode with its divisions of strophe and antistrophe. It was also at this time that the term "lyric" first came into use. The Greeks who were Aristotle's contemporaries made three fundamental distinctions. Elegiac and iambic poems were chanted; melic or lyric poems were sung by one voice to musical accompaniment (the lyre), and choric was for several voices. Notice that the distinctions were based on external differences and not subject matter. Eventually, "lyric" became a general name for any poem that was composed for singing, and the meaning did not change until the Renaissance.

In the lyric there is a basic tension between words and music. Although both are temporal forms, always throwing the attention forward, because words have semantic properties we are tempted (at some times more than others) to stop and think about them; meanwhile the song's melody and rhythm continue to hurtle us on. In addition, there is a basic division in the function of these two components of the lyric. Some critics maintain that the words convey ideas and the music conveys emotion. Others differentiate between the intellectual appeal of music and that of poetry, saying that the former is more related to structure and the latter to content. Whatever the differences of critical opinion as to what the separate functions are, the tension caused by their separateness is generally agreed upon. The ideal lyric profits from this tension, keeping a balance between the weight of the two.

In the primitive lyric the problem of conflict did not exist, since (as we mentioned earlier), the two forms were thought of as a fused unit, and within that unit they not only complemented each other but depended on each other for survival. As each art became more developed, however, the problem of rivalry arose. Words became music in themselves, music attempted to express ideas on its own—one began to outshine the other in virtuosity. In almost all lyric periods, one or the other form has been to some degree subordinated. During the Greek era, for example, the odes of Pindar and Bacchylides, the music was obviously subordinated to the words. The Elizabethan period, the great age of English lyricism, was a time when, at least in the early part, words and music were written in careful consideration of each other, either by the same artist or by joint contribution of the poet and composer. But the Renaissance brought with it a separation that has lasted for centuries and that has created the hybrid form known as lyrical poetry.

Several events combined in the Renaissance to produce breaches that affected the entire fabric of society and culture and, in turn, the lyric. In the latter part of the Elizabethan period the once nearly symbiotic relationship between poetry and music grew apart. During the late Middle Ages, music had become more sophisticated and was finally able to stand on its own. We can see a marked evolution in the difference between the simple music of the early Elizabethan lutanist, in which the composer was chiefly concerned with conveying the poet's meaning, and the complex patterns of the later madrigals, which were concerned chiefly with the music and which often drowned the words in complicated fugal progressions. So too with poetry. The poet grew weary of the rhyme, the refrain, the end stops, the exact stanza form of the lyric. All these things had once stimulated his art; now he felt shackled by them. Poetry too was becoming more sophisticated and profound. The complex analogies of metaphysical verse required an intellectual analysis, but the temporal experience of song prohibits such lingering. John Donne's poetry, for example, demands reading and rereading. This brings us to a crucial point.

The invention of printing completely altered life in the Renaissance and in each succeeding age. It created the literate society, brought us out of the Dark Ages (the ages of magic, by the way), and spread uniformed knowledge and culture across the world. Marshall

McLuhan, in *Understanding Media*, and more exhaustively in *The Gutenberg Galaxy*, explained the changes that the medium of print itself effected because of the kind of perspective it demanded (and still demands) from its audience.

Let's review the points that most concern our topic. First, printed, mass-produced books encouraged individualism and the fixed, personal, detached point of view. A book is an artifact. A person can open it or shut it. He can take it to his room to read (indeed, printing even changed architecture, demanding that houses have separate, closed-off rooms that one could go to in order to read his book). Since under normal circumstances books are read individually and privately, the reader's response is individual and private. Thus the communal quality of poetry was lost.

Also the medium is "hot"; it provides a large amount of specific information—information that can be reread as often as desired— thereby precluding the involvement that an oral form required, eliminating the sense of mystery necessary for the survival of magic, urging in, eventually, the Age of Reason. The linear form encouraged linear perspective and linear thought, which nurtured logic and scientific methodology. The line, which was segmented into separate words and separate letters, encouraged fragmentation. The mechanical age was now prepared for, with all its assembly lines and wheels and gadgets.

Since print dictated that poetry be seen and not heard, poets began suiting their work to a visual rather than an auditory medium. Because of its strict pattern and traditionally conventional content, poetry written for music is usually monotonous to read. The rhyme and refrain become wearisome. Sometimes a verbal rhythm seems lopsided when read, although it is even when put to the appropriate music. The poet Dryden once complained, "I have been obliged to cramp my verses, and make them rugged to the reader, that they may be harmonious to the hearer." And so, as a result of all these conflicts, the sister arts went their separate ways. Consequently, although poets continued to be more or less knowledgeable about music, their knowledge resulted more from social contacts than from any close ties between the arts. Moreover, the gulf between them grew wider with time.

The advent of printing intensified another oncoming divorce. The minstrel was shoved out of his position as a disseminator of verse, as poems of all kinds became readily available in print. Also we begin to see a definitive split during this period between high and low art, or between art and folk. In the realm of the lyric, there was a growing distinction between the art or literarary lyric and the folk lyric. From the close of the Renaissance the folk lyric continued to flourish on its own, however, through the days of the broadsheets and chapbooks, through the Victorian street ballads, the vaudeville and Broadway music halls, to the pop songs of our time. Its illiteracy has always been preserved; the folk lyric has been virtually unaffected by the literary fashion of the day. Usually, however, somewhat more influence has been felt the other way. Sophisticated poets from Swift to Eliot have at times borrowed the street manner for their poems.

The art lyric traveled another path. Except for Dryden, after the early seventeenth century no major English poet until Robert Burns spent a large part of his poetic efforts writing songs that were intended for singing. Although poets continued to create many poems that were called "songs" and odes to music (plenty of them in the eighteenth century), most poets were not interested in its possibilities for poetry. Moreover, few poets besides Milton, Ireland's Thom Moore, and Gerard Manley Hopkins could claim any solid musical training. Moore and Burns, both excellent lyricists, stand out in the English poetic tradition, which was veering further and further away from song. The neoclassic couplet, for example, was about the most unsuitable verse for music in the history of poetry. And, finally, the decline in drama also influenced the lyric's decline, since so many of the best songs had been written for the stage. In 1798, *Lyrical Ballads*, though attempting to return poetry to "real" speech, never approached bringing it back to song. The lyric had become the lyric*al*. The subject and tone defined the poem. The term "lyric" no longer referred specifically to a song-poem, but rather to a particular

ﾌ poetry that was, as the poet William Wordsworth defined it, ﾍ ﾍnotion recollected in tranquillity."

To emphasize the essential features of a strain that has undoubtedly influenced the writers represented here, let's take additional liberties with time and space. The following have played important roles in the completion of a lyric cycle.

William Blake renewed the concept of the poet as magic-maker, as shaman. His association of the poem with a mystical experience recurs in the works of such spiritual-minded poets as Hopkins, Baudelaire, Yeats, and Rilke. Also, Blake's "Songs of Innocence and Experience" (for which he reputedly had composed melodies that he sang to himself), in their blending of a simple, lyrical surface with deeper levels of mystery, allegory, and archetype, were ideal models for many of our current lyrics. Compare Blake's "Songs," for example, with Dylan's songs on his *John Wesley Harding* album.

Edgar Allan Poe, in his subordination of thought to the music of his words, and in his concept and use of the grotesque, had a considerable influence on all of modern poetry. Much of his influence was directly absorbed and then rebounded by the *fin de siècle* French symbolist poets, especially Mallarmé and Valéry, who consciously aspired to produce in poetry the pure and absolute qualities of music.

The French surrealists, for whom André Breton was a chief spokesman, liberated the unconscious in poetry and for poetry. Among themselves they tried experiments invoking the creative unconscious in the spontaneous "automatic poem," and seeking to collect their creative consciousness in the communal "group poem."

During the twenties in America and elsewhere there was much experimental activity in poetry. E. E. Cummings was in the vanguard of this activity, and in his verse we can see the seeds of two divergent strains in poetry. His concern with the formal and spatial arrangement of words (and parts of words) on the page helped to precipitate the concrete movement. Much of this poetry is not merely dependent on but is restricted to a visual orientation. Hence Ginsberg's reference to "abstract voiceless page."

On the other hand, Cummings was very much concerned with

the oral form. Many of his visual patterns were aids to oral delivery, and he even made commercial recordings of his own poetry, as many poets have done since. These recordings gave him an infinitely greater listening audience, just as the invention of printing gave the Renaissance poet an infinitely greater reading audience. The differences between the two kinds of audience, as we have mentioned earlier, are significant. And it was the new electric technology that helped to create a new audience or rather, to recreate the audience in its primitive form.

The media of records, radio, television, and film have redirected our orientation toward the spoken and sung word. For example, electronic amplification is one factor in making rock concerts the huge communal gatherings that they are, since it enables the sound to be carried over large areas. These concerts are often recorded and filmed, so they can be replayed to other group audiences. The impact of these new media, and the involvement they demand, is total and continuous. Many observers feel that they are replacing the printed word, that society has become (or at least is still in the process of becoming) postliterate and thereby postliterary. Electric circuitry, McLuhan tells us, has become modern society's central nervous system. We share via radio and television the everyday experiences of our African and Asian brothers. We are rapidly becoming, in a sense, all members of the same tribe, living in a "global village."

The new media made poets more interested in public readings. In America, the beat movement of the fifties accelerated this interest; readings developed into true communal experiences, complete with chanting and incantations. And once again, the emphasis was on performance, with poems often improvised and spontaneous. Kenneth Patchen and others tried experiments—live and on radio and records—with poetry read to a jazz background, and although the relationship between the two forms was at best contrapuntal, the effort was another major step toward the final fusion and return to song and song forms. As certain jazz forms are heavy influences on current rock music, the beats are the immediate poetic forbears of the current lyric movement.

Pop art has provided another kind of fusion. The pop revolution has proved to be a great cultural equalizer. Be it music, movies, painting, sculpture, or commercial art, pop has consistently shattered traditional boundaries between the sophisticated and the mundane, the art and the folk, the classical and the camp. A Dylan song called "Tombstone Blues" has Ma Rainey and Beethoven composing a song together. "Bob Dylan's 115th Dream" mixes various literary, historical and mythological sources in an absurd modern account of the discovery of America. The Beatles' songs and their bankbooks offer collective proof that there need be no distinction between art and public entertainment. Nor is there as much need for conscious cross-fertilization between sophisticated poetry and folk song, nor between culture and subcultures, as the global village becomes a tighter and tighter unit.

Dylan's work in the sixties heralded poetry's return to song and song forms. His songs were ingenious combinations of blues rhythms, surreal imagery, topical protest, fatalistic existentialism, a huge repertory of poetic devices, and colorful verbal idiom. His impact on the pop music scene is undeniable; he made so many musicians conscious of infusing their songs with poetry. But equally important, he has made a growing number of poets aware of the new possibilities of poetry and music together. A milieu, nurtured in the sixties, is now established. Leonard Cohen, already a successful novelist and linear poet, is writing songs and recording them personally. Ed Sanders and Tuli Kupferberg of the Fugs, both linear poets, both incorporate their verses into song, as did Richard Fariña. These poets are by no means ignorant of the literary tradition, but neither do they have to *borrow* the street idiom. Poets and musicians meet in Liverpool, in New York, in San Francisco, and blend their wares.

A significant number of the lyric writers whose works appear in this book have written their own music and performed their own songs. Donovan is perhaps the best current example of both the primitive mystic poet and the early Renaissance minstrel poet. And he and Dylan and the others are reaching (through the electric circuits) millions of young people, some of whom are budding bards themselves. In his excellent study of the lyric, *The Lyric Impulse,* C. Day Lewis commented on this contemporary phenomenon:

"The mantle of the bard has fallen upon the shoulders of the pop singer—from which it is frequently torn off by a raving horde of his fans and distributed among them as souvenirs. Nothing new in this. The first pop singer, Orpheus, was torn in pieces by Maenads. And dare we feel superior about these rabid manifestations? Do they not indicate a psychological need, a spontaneity of emotion, which the higher levels of art in the West are today ignoring?"

> C. Day Lewis, *The Lyric Impulse* (Cambridge: Harvard University Press, 1965), p.2.

The minstrel has returned; his stringed instrument is now electric, and without traveling he can be heard across the world. And he will be heard—by everyone—since the human ear is not equipped with earlids.

Thus a cycle seems to be reaching completion. We are now in a position to consider again the questions raised earlier: Will the current lyric movement be a major direction? Is it new? In view of the increasingly large dimensions of the lyric movement, there can be no doubt that it is, by sheer force of numbers, a major trend. The return to the roots of poetry demonstrated by the reemergence of the singer-poet makes this movement, in an even more significant sense, a major direction.

But as these two questions are answered, two further problems can be anticipated concerning the proposed cyclical theory, and so it must be clarified. One, we cannot say that *all* poetry is returning to song; as long as people continue to speak, there will be spoken poetry. As T. S. Eliot once warned, if poetry departs too far from common speech, it can wither and die of abstraction. We can propose, however, that the lyric movement is a major direction. And this brings up the second problem.

If the mainstream of poetry is returning to lyric form, and the lyric is by tradition a light, simple song, then what happens to poetry that is by nature sophisticated, complex, and profound? We spoke earlier of the tension between the forward-moving musical pace and the words whose meanings must sometimes be pondered. To preserve the balance, the lyric has traditionally been light and simple in meaning and thereby fast-moving. Although most current lyrics continue to be light, several important songs point toward a new kind of lyric. Dylan's "All Along the Watchtower" is one example. The song has a simple narrative surface that moves along quickly but, in the style of Blake, it uses symbol, allegory, and archetype to suggest more profound meanings. Songs like Phil Ochs' "Crucifixion," Carl Oglesby's "Black Panther," Fariña's "Celebration for a Grey Day," and Dylan's "Sad-Eyed Lady of the Lowlands" are examples of a somewhat different type. These songs, with their intricate image patterns, their many-sided symbols and levels of meaning, are "heavy." They do not offer a contrast to the "higher levels of art."

And yet they are rapid. In each song the music keeps us moving toward the conclusion. We cannot linger on the "meaning"; lingering is for later. In this electric age, things happen allatonce, and, sometimes, if we are to survive, we must let them happen and reflect on them later. So with the films of Fellini and Godard, so with the Joshua Light Show, so with "Sad-Eyed Lady of the Lowlands."

Still another possible explanation of the "heavy" lyric bears consideration. It may be that the electronic media are gradually conditioning us to the ability to respond to many different stimuli on many levels. As we continue to experience the perceptual expansion that the electronic media stimulate, it is possible that our ability to function simultaneously on the perceptual and intellectual levels will increase. Modern film techniques overwhelm us with a rapid series of visual images, while contemporary songs bombard us with an infinitely complex fusion of visual, auditory, and kinetic images and intellectual ideas.

These modern orphic voices are plugging us in to the times we actually live in.

CHAPTER TWO

I and Thou

love

unlove

one

two

29224

WIDOW WITH SHAWL (a portrait)
Donovan Leitch

dear wind that shakes the barley free
blow home my true love's ship to me
fill her sails i aweary wait upon the shore

forsake her not in times of storm
protect her oaken beams from harm
fill her sail i aweary wait upon the shore

whether he be in Africa
or deep asleep in India
fill his dreams i aweary wait upon the shore

seven years and seven days
no man has seen my woman ways dear God i aweary
wait upon the shore

and in my chariot of sleep
i ride the vast and dreamy deep deep sea
i awake aweary on the shore

dear snow white gulls upon the wing
i, like you, am lamenting
for my love i aweary cry upon the shore

along the shingle beach i go
the wind about me as i make my way
to my weary dream upon my bed

1. Why is the poem called a portrait? How much of the poem is visual? What is the subject of the portrait—a woman or a feeling?

2. What are the relationships between the refrain and the lines that precede it in each stanza? What are the effects of the subtle changes in the line as it is repeated? Do you think the repetition of the line increases the emotional impact of the song?

3. Consider all the implications of the word "dream" as it is used in the song. In stanza three particularly, how does the word, momentarily at least, reunite husband and wife?

4. Which images are also symbols? In the context of the poem, is the wind male or female? Is it destructive or creative? Read Shelley's "Ode to the West Wind." Any parallels?

5. Compare this to an Anglo-Saxon poem entitled "The Wanderer." Consider the term "elegiac" as it applies to each poem. Could the two poems in any way constitute a dialogue?

6. Seven years and seven days: after this period of time elapses, a missing person can be pronounced legally dead. Thus a woman whose husband has been missing for that period of time is now a widow and now free to marry. Is this woman free?

7. Seven years, seven days, seven stanzas in the poem—what special symbolic properties does the number "seven" have?

SAD-EYED LADY OF THE LOWLANDS
Bob Dylan

With your mercury mouth in the missionary times
And your eyes like smoke and your prayers like rhymes
And your silver cross and your voice like chimes
Oh, who among them do they think could bury you?
With your pockets well-protected at last
And your streetcar visions which you place on the grass
And your flesh like silk and your face like glass
Who among them could they get to carry you?

Sad-eyed lady of the lowlands
Where the sad-eyed prophet says that no man comes
My warehouse eyes my Arabian drums
Should I leave them by your gate
Or sad-eyed lady, should I wait?

With your sheets like metal and your belt like lace
And your deck of cards missing the jack and the ace
And your basement clothes and your hollow face
Who among them can think he could outguess you?
With your silhouette when the sunlight dims
Into your eyes where the moonlight swims
And your matchbook songs and your gypsy hymns
Who among them would try to impress you?

Sad-eyed lady of the lowlands
Where the sad-eyed prophet says that no man comes

My warehouse eyes my Arabian drums
Should I leave them by your gate
Or, sad-eyed lady, should I wait?

The kings of Tyrus with their convict list
Are waiting in line for their geranium kiss
And you wouldn't know it would happen like this
But who among them really wants just to kiss you
With your childhood flames on your midnight rug
And your Spanish manners and your mother's drugs
And your cowboy mouth and your curfew plugs
Who among them do you think could resist you?

Sad-eyed lady of the lowlands
Where the sad-eyed prophet says that no man comes
My warehouse eyes my Arabian drums
Should I leave them by your gate
Or, sad-eyed lady, should I wait?

Oh, the farmers and the businessmen they all did decide
To show you the dead angels that they used to hide
But why did they pick you to sympathize with their side
How could they ever mistake you?
They wish you'd accepted the blame for the farm,
But with the sea at your feet and the phony false alarm
And with the child of a hoodlum wrapped up in your arms,
How could they ever have persuaded you?

Sad-eyed lady of the lowlands
Where the sad-eyed prophet says that no man comes
My warehouse eyes my Arabian drums
Should I leave them by your gate
Or, sad-eyed lady, should I wait?

With your sheet metal memory of Cannery Row
And your magazine husband who one day just had to go
And your gentleness now which you just can't help but show
Who among them do you think would employ you?
Now, you stand with your thief; you're on his parole
With your holy medallion which your fingertips fold
And your saint-like face and your ghost-like soul
Who among them could ever think he could destroy you?

Sad-eyed lady of the lowlands
Where the sad-eyed prophet says that no man comes
My warehouse eyes my Arabian drums
Should I leave them by your gate
Or, sad-eyed lady, should I wait?

Marcel Duchamp, "Nude Descending a Staircase," No. 2, 1912. Oils on canvas 58 x 35 inches. Philadelphia Museum of Art: Louise and Walter Arensberg Collection, '50-134-59.

NU DESCENDANT UN ESCALIER

1. Speaking of portraits . . . compare this song with Marcel Duchamp's "Nude Descending a Staircase, No. 2." What is cubism? Can it be a literary (poetic) style?

2. William Faulkner said of his novel, *The Sound and the Fury,* that each time he finished writing the story he realized that it wasn't complete, and so he started over again at the beginning and from another perspective. Thus the four-part structure of the book. One story, four stories. How does this relate to Dylan's song?

3. Mercury mouth?! Cowboy mouth?! Are you tempted to try to interpret this song? How many of all these metaphors do you respond to somehow immediately? Which ones leave you blank? Now give them some thought. Compare your responses with others. Does the nature of a response to a metaphor (or an image) depend more on an individual's background and past experiences than on the metaphor (or image) itself?

4. What is the relationship between the warehouse and the Arabian drums? Is there a contrast running through the poem between the exotic and the mundane? The line that contains these words appeared in print two ways. In Richard Goldstein's *The Poetry of Rock* (p. 77) it reads—"My warehouse has my Arabian drums"; but in the *Blonde on Blonde* Songbook (Deluxe ed., p. 47) it says—"My warehouse eyes my Arabian drums." Listen to Dylan singing the line and see if you can figure out which is correct. Does it matter? Which version do you like better? Whose song is this, anyway?

5. Look in Marshall McLuhan's *Understanding Media* to find out what he means by a "hot" medium and a "cool" medium. Is the recording of "Sad-Eyed Lady" hot or cool? Is the song in print hot or cool? Are heat and cold relative or absolute qualities? Do these questions have any relation to the questions under number four?

6. Discuss pagan-Christian imagery. Who is the Sad-Eyed Lady? What comments are made on religion? Is this song iconoclastic?

AS TEARS GO BY

Mick Jagger, Keith Richard, and Andrew Loog Oldham

It is the evening of the day
I sit and watch the chidren play
Smiling faces I can see
But not for me
I sit and watch as tears go by.

My riches can't buy everything
I want to hear the children sing
All I hear is the sound
Of rain falling on the ground
I sit and watch as tears go by.

It is the evening of the day
I sit and watch the children play
Doing things I used to do
They think are new
I sit and watch as tears go by.

1. What is the literal statement of the poem? Does the poem make any comment other than on the surface level?

2. How much of the poem's effect depends on what is *not* said? Try to explain what is not said.

3. How do images function in the poem to establish tone? How does the refrain affect tone?

4. Notice that the overwhelming majority of the poem's words are monosyllabic. What contribution does this make to tone? To meaning?

5. Read W. B. Yeats' "Sailing to Byzantium." Compare and contrast the two poems. How do the first two stanzas, in particular, of Yeats' poem relate to "As Tears Go By"?

PEOPLE ARE STRANGE

Jim Morrison

People are strange when you're a stranger,
Faces look ugly when you're alone
Women seem wicked when you're unwanted,
Streets are uneven when you're down.
When you're strange
Faces come out of the rain
When you're strange
No one remembers your name
When you're strange
When you're strange
When you're strange.

1. Is this poem about loneliness or about alienation? Is there a difference?

2. Is the poem an interior monologue?

3. Does the word "when" signify time, or condition, or causality?

4. What's in a name? Read *Nobody Knows My Name*, by James Baldwin (1960), or *The Invisible Man*, by Ralph Ellison (1952). In any of the novels that you've read, is the central character ever unnamed? What is the point? Consider the full significance of a name.

5. What is the effect of repetition? If it's available, listen to The Doors' recording. How do the voice and style accentuate the effect?

HEY, THAT'S NO WAY TO SAY GOODBYE

Leonard Cohen

I loved you in the morning
Our kisses deep and warm,
Your head upon the pillow
Like a sleepy golden storm.
Yes, many loved before us
I know that we are not new,
In city and in forest
They smiled like me and you,
But now it's come to distances
And both of us must try,
Your eyes are soft with sorrow,
Hey, that's no way to say goodbye.

I'm not looking for another
As I wander in my time,
Walk me to the corner
Our steps will always rhyme,
You know my love goes with you
As your love stays with me,
It's just the way it changes
Like the shoreline and the sea,
But let's not talk of love or chains
And things we can't untie,
Your eyes are soft with sorrow,
Hey, that's no way to say goodbye.

I loved you in the morning
Our kisses deep and warm,
Your head upon the pillow
Like a sleepy golden storm.

Yes, many loved before us
I know that we are not new,
In city and in forest
They smiled like me and you,
But let's not talk of love or chains
And things we can't untie,
Your eyes are soft with sorrow,
Hey, that's no way to say goodbye.

1. Make up a character sketch of each of the two lovers, speculating from any evidences in the song of their different approaches to saying goodbye. What would you suppose their romance was like?

2.   Your head upon the pillow
        Like a sleepy golden storm.

        . . . .

        It's just the way it changes
        Like the shoreline and the sea,

   What are these devices called? What is their general function in a poem? (Compare your answer to this question with the answers of other people.) Examine each of these two "devices" and evaluate the contribution of each to the total effect of the poem. Do the separate "meanings" of each couplet approach each other in any way?

3. What other metaphorical "devices" are used in the song? What would it sound like without them? Strip the poem down to its barest statement.

4. (Why) is it important that many have loved before them?

HOW LONG

Tim Hardin

How long, how long
has the evenin' train been gone?
Baby, won't you tell me how long

I'm ridin' a railroad
I've headed out of town.

The way things is
It don't look like I ought ta hang around.

1. Is the time of day symbolic?

2. How "is" things? The poem gives an impression, inviting our imaginations to complete the picture. How would you complete it? Is the situation between the two lovers a familiar one? How do the speaker's words compare with the parting words of the speaker in Leonard Cohen's "Hey, That's No Way to Say Goodbye"?

3. Consider the train as a symbol, first as a natural symbol (by its shape, power, etc.) and then as a cultural symbol. Do both figure in the context of the song?

4. Think of all the poems and songs (especially blues songs) that tell of "traveling men." The wanderer is an archetypal figure, appearing again and again in myth, folktale, and literature. Why do you think this is so? What would you say are the inside and outside forces that make someone a wanderer? Do these forces differ from culture to culture?

5. Notice the grammatical and spelling irregularities. Is this the blues idiom?

6. This song provides us with an excellent opportunity to contrast media. In print, the poem is brief, bare, and impressionistic, but would you say that it is not an aesthetic whole? If a recording is available, listen to Tim Hardin sing his song. Does the singer's voice fill in gaps for you? Is performance *absolutely* necessary to project the full "meaning" of the words? Do you think that performance is more necessary for a blues song than for an ordinary pop song? Than for a poem?

SPOONFUL

Willie Dixon

It could be a spoonful of diamonds,
Could be a spoonful of gold,
Just a little spoon of your precious love
Satisfies my soul.
Men lies about it,
Some of them cries about it,
Some of them dies about it,
Ev'rything fight about a spoonful,
That spoon, that spoon, that spoonful.

It could be a spoonful of coffee,
Could be a spoonful of tea,
But a little spoon of your precious love
Is good enough for me.
Men lies about it,
Some of them cries about it,
Some of them dies about it,
Ev'rything fight about a spoonful,
That spoon, that spoon, that spoonful.

It could be a spoonful of water,
Saved from the desert sand,
But one spoon of them forty fives
Saved from another man.
Men lies about it,
Some of them cries about it,
Some of them dies about it,
Ev'rything fight about a spoonful,
That spoon, that spoon, that spoonful.

1. Notice again, as in "How Long," the unsophisticated diction. "Spoonful" is
   another blues song, by Willie Dixon, one of the great blues men. Is this song
   another indication of a special language of the blues, or do you think this
   kind of diction is part of the entire folk tradition?

   You might like to try this experiment. Take a few examples of blues lyrics.
   (Paul Oliver has a large selection in his book, *Blues Fell This Morning,* 1960.
   Eric Sackheim has compiled an even more comprehensive volume in *The
   Blues Line,* 1969.) If possible, obtain lyrics to songs you will be able to hear
   on records. Then imagine you are an especially pedantic English teacher and
   submit the lyrics to a careful grammatical scrutiny. Once the songs are
   "corrected," try singing (or reading) them. Has the meaning changed?

2. The word "spoonful" is loaded to begin with. Consult a good dictionary of
   slang to find its reference to the drug scene. But each time it is used in the
   song it adds associations. Remember Eliot's line in "The Love Song of
   J. Alfred Prufrock," "I have measured out my life with coffee spoons."
   Contrast the use in each poem of the word's connotations.

3. "Spoonful" is a very popular song among blues and rock musicians. It has
   been recorded, with various arrangements, by several different groups and
   individuals (some versions of the song are listed in the discography at the end
   of the book). It might be interesting to do a comparative study of these
   versions, focusing on the possible effect of musical arrangement and vocal
   emphasis on the meaning of the words.

I GIVE YOU THE MORNING

Tom Paxton

Ever again the morning creeps
Across your shoulder.
Through the frosted window pane
The sun grows bolder.
Your hair flows down your pillow,
You're still dreaming,
    I think I'll wake you now and hold you,
    Tell you again the things I told you,
    Behold, I give you the morning,
    I give you the day.

Through the waving curtain wall
The sun is streaming.
Far behind your flickering eyelids
You're still dreaming.
You're dreaming of the good times,
And you're smiling.
    I think I'll wake you now and hold you,
    Tell you again the things I told you.
    Behold, I give you the morning,
    I give you the day.

Close beneath our window sill,
The earth is humming.
Like an eager Christmas child,
The day is coming.
Listen to the morning song
It's singing.
    I think I'll wake you now and hold you.
    Tell you again the things I told you.

Behold, I give you the morning,
I give you the day.

Like an antique ballroom fan,
Your eyelids flutter.
Sunlight streams across your eyes
Through open shutter.
Now I think you're ready for the journey.
I think I'll wake you now and hold you,
Tell you again the things I told you.
Behold, I give you the morning,
I give you the day.

1. Defend one or all of these impressions. Are they valid?

He is speaking to his bride the morning after their first night together.

He is speaking to his mistress on one of many mornings. This is a part of his ritual, like the cock who raises the sun each day.

He is about to kill her sending her on "the journey."

He has killed her, and he is retreating into a wish-fantasy that her death is only sleep.

He is alone, talking to himself, like Eben Flood in E. A. Robinson's poem, "Mr. Flood's Party."

He is about to break off the relationship with the girl.

She is "coming down" from a drug experience.

He is about to take her on a drug experience.

The poem deals with the advent of a religious experience.

Upon what criteria did you base your defense?

2. Walls and windows, skin and eyes; how deep can the sunlight penetrate?

MOONCHILD

Robert Fripp, Ian McDonald, Greg Lake, Michael Giles, Peter Sinfield

Call her moonchild
Dancing in the shallows of a river
Lonely moonchild
Dreaming in the shadow of the willow.

Talking to the trees of the
    cobweb strange
Sleeping on the steps of a fountain
Waving silver wands to the
    night-birds song
Waiting for the sun on the mountain.

She's a moonchild
Gathering the flowers in a garden.
Lovely moonchild
Drifting on the echoes of the hours

Sailing on the wind
    in a milk white gown
Dropping circle stones on a sun dial
Playing hide and seek
    with the ghosts of a dawn
Waiting for a smile from a sun child.

1. What is the poem's literal statement?

2. Consider the poem in terms of image. How many images of change and impermanence can you find? Compare this poem with W. B. Yeats' "The Song of Wandering Aengus." How many similarities of image can you find? Aengus wakes up to the bitter knowledge of mortality and his isolation. What will happen to the moonchild when she wakes?

3. Consider these three shapes in reference to the poem:

   Which shape fits best? Why? Draw your own shape to express your feelings about the song.

4. Consider the moon and the sun as symbols. Why is the moon female and the sun male?

CELEBRATION FOR A GREY DAY
Richard Fariña

Be quiet now and still. Be unafraid:
That hiss and garden tinkle is the rain,
That face you saw breathe on the window pane
Was just a startled cat with eyes of jade—
Cats worry in the rain, you know, and are afraid.
The nervous laugh that creeps into our room
Is throated in a voice beyond the door.
We hear it once and then no more,
A distant echo tumbling from its loom.
Our time is measured in another room.

We know days pass away because we're told.
We lie alone and sense the reeling earth.
(You whisper in my ear it had some worth)
And I learn to keep you from the cold.
There are so many things that must be told.
I speak of lost regimes and distant times,
And mooneyed children whirling in the womb,
And legless beggars prophesying doom,
And afternoons of rain spun into rhyme.
(The patter of the rainfall marks our time.)

As does the waning moon. Or muted sun.
As do the nodding gods who ride the sea.
For even now, alone and still with me,
You sense the bonds that cannot be undone:
Our pulse is in the rain and moon and sun,
We take our breaths together and are one.

1. The speaker in the poem is trying to comfort the girl he loves. Why is she afraid? Why is he not afraid? How is the cat related to her fears?

2. What is the significance of the adjectives that precede earth, moon, sun, and gods?

3. Notice the tension between the references to time going by and to timelessness. What purpose does this tension serve?

4. This poem has a carefully worked out rhyme scheme. Does the rhyme contribute to your response to the poem? Do you find it pleasing? Does the rhyme give a musical effect to the song? Does it have a thematic function?

SINCE YOU'VE ASKED

Judy Collins

What I'll give you, since you've asked,
Is all my time together
Take the rugged sunny days
The warm and rocky weather
Take the roads that I have walked along
Looking for tomorrow's time, peace of mind

As my life spills into yours
Changing with the hours
Filling up the world with time
Turning time to flowers
I can show you all the songs
That I never sang to one man before

We have seen a million stones
Lying by the water
You have climbed the hills with me
To the mountain shelter
Taken off the days one by one
Setting them to breathe in the sun

Take the lilies and the lace
From the days of childhood
All the willow winding paths
Leading up and outward
This is what I give
This is what I ask you for, nothing more

This poem is a response, partly an answer, to Judy Collins' poem.

I'll give you rainwashed streets
    and bright new pennies
Leaf boats sailing in the gutter
    the piercing smell of April

I'll give you the sound of insects
    fields panting in the sun
Heavy with the threat of harvest
    the shimmering air of August

I'll give you the smell of burning leaves
    crisp apples green and slightly bitter
Nights trembling with the hint of frost
    the cold winds of November

I'll give you pensive hours of questioning
    and the blank face of solitude
Empty packages tied with satin ribbons
    the sting of sleet

1. Compare the two poems. What differences do you see in the two speakers' approaches to the experience of love? Which one is willing to give more? Which one is willing to risk more?

2. Poets so often express the feeling of love through images and metaphors, something concrete that both lovers can share, yet personal for both of them. What images and metaphors would you choose to express your love?

3.   Looking for tomorrow's time

. . . .
As my life spills into yours
Changing with the hours

. . . .
Taken off the days one by one
April . . . August . . . November . . . the sting of sleet

Why are love poems so often concerned with time?

SUPERGIRL

Tuli Kupferberg

I want a girl that can _ _ _ _ like an angel
Cook like the devil
Swing like a dancer
Work like a pony
Dream like a poet
Flow like a mountain stream

Supergirl
Supergirl
Supergirl

I want a girl that can kiss like a cherry
Squeeze like a berry
Smell like an orchard
Talk like a songbird
Walk like a fountain
Touch like a flower
Sing like the leaves of grass

Supergirl
Supergirl
Supergirl
My Supergirl

I want a girl that can love like a monkey
Hug like a castle
Think like a darling
Lap like a lemon
Eat like a monster
Roll like a jug of wine

Supergirl

1. What is the poetic device the poem is built around? Compare its use with the technique in Bob Dylan's "Sad-Eyed Lady of the Lowlands." Would you say that each poem depicts a kind of goddess? What kind?

2. Contrast the mood and tone of this poem with "Since You've Asked." What differences are there in the kind of love the two speakers want?

3. Notice the open space in the first line. Can you fill in the blank? The specific word was deleted to "preserve common decency." How much of an aesthetic blow does this kind of surgery inflict?

SPANISH HARLEM

Phil Spector and Jerry Leiber

There is a rose in Spanish Harlem,
A red rose up in Spanish Harlem.
It is a special one;
It's never seen the sun,
It only comes out when the moon is on the run
And all the stars are gleaming.
It's growing in the street
Right up through the concrete
But soft and sweet and dreaming.

There is a rose in Spanish Harlem,
A red rose up in Spanish Harlem
With eyes as black as coal
That look down in my soul
And start a fire there and then I lose control.
I have to beg your pardon,
I'm going to pick that rose
And watch her as she grows in my garden.

1. A partial symbology of the rose:

> Take thou this Rose, O Rose,
> Since love's own flower it is
> And by that rose
> Thy lover captive is.
> > (trans. from anon. Medieval Latin lyric)

> Just as the unblemished rose
> Exists among sharp thorns
> So the mistress of my heart
> Exists among sharp tongues
> > (Trans. from anon. Medieval French Lyric)

> Gather ye rosebuds while ye may.
> > (Robert Herrick)

> THE SICK ROSE

> O rose, thou art sick!
> The invisible worm
> That flies in the night
> In the howling storm,

> Has found out thy bed
> Of crimson joy
> And his dark secret love
> Does thy life destroy.
> > (William Blake)

> But when the melancholy fit shall fall
> > Sudden from heaven like a weeping cloud,
> That fosters the droop-headed flowers all,
> > And hides the green hill in an April shroud;
> Then glut thy sorrow on a morning rose, ...
> > (from John Keats, "Ode on Melancholy")

> a rose is a rose is a rose
> > (Gertrude Stein)

Writers and poets from Sappho to these current songs have dwelt on the symbolic properties of the rose. Moreover, as our great twentieth century writers, Yeats, Eliot, and Joyce, will attest, poets have found uniquely personal ways of using it in their works. Barbara Seward's *The Symbolic Rose* is an illuminating study of the evolution of the rose as symbol in literature. It might be interesting to inquire into this area since, as the author states, "a history of the rose becomes a history of symbolism."

2. What sharp contrasts are being drawn in the poem?

3. Can you identify the various ways in which metaphor works in the poem?

SALLY, GO 'ROUND THE ROSES

Zel Sanders and Lona Stevens

Sally, go 'round the roses.
Sally, go 'round the roses.
Sally, go 'round the roses.
Sally, go 'round the pretty roses.

Roses, they can't hurt you.
The Roses, they can't hurt you.
Roses, they can't hurt you.
No, the roses, they can't hurt you.

Sally, don'tcha go, don'tcha go downtown.
Sally, don'tcha go, don'tcha go downtown.
Saddest thing in this whole wide world
Is to see your baby with another girl.

Sally, go 'round the roses.
Sally, go 'round the roses.
Sally, go 'round the roses.
Sally, go 'round the pretty roses.

They won't tell your secrets.
They won't tell your secrets.
They won't tell your secrets.
No, the roses won't tell your secrets.

Sally, baby, cry; let your hair hang down.
Sally, baby, cry; let your hair hang down.
Sit and cry where the roses grow,
You can sit and cry and not a soul will know.

Sally, go 'round the roses.

1. What effect does the continued repetition have? Do you see any similarities between the repeated lines and the following lines from a nursery rhyme?

> Here we go 'round the mulberry bush
> the mulberry bush
> the mulberry bush
> Here we go 'round the mulberry bush
> So early in the morning.

Near the song's end, Sally is referred to as "baby." What kind of an experience can we assume she has recently had? Could her reaction to this experience be a regression to childhood?

2. The chief dichotomy operating in the poem is "roses" versus "downtown." Downtown is that archetypal evil place (it is in the same direction as hell), while the roses presumably are part of a garden. As opposed to the evils of downtown, the garden is suggestive of the archetypal garden of paradise, an innocent and (theoretically) safe place. But what particular qualities are associated with the roses in this poem? Is Sally's garden more of an asylum than a paradise?

3. "Let your hair hang down" is an idiomatic expression with a few different interpretations. Which is being used here?

MISS LONELY (Are You Blue?)

Eric Anderson

Oh, the night has sent you out for lovin',
And the day finds you back out runnin'
As dawn becomes the lovers' enemy,
And you hope perhaps you can find
Someone that won't leave you behind
A victim of life's sad mystery.

    Oh, oh, come on, you can step inside,
    The stairs won't follow you, if you hide
    The walls won't even ask you why.
    Miss Lonely, are you blue tonight?

Parks and subways people sittin'
With their faces where you see nothin' written
Look up, look down or wander nervously
With their eyes that find no place for restin'
And their thoughts that only leave you guessin'
You know there ain't a face here that could ever set you free.

    Oh, oh come on, you can step inside,
    The stairs won't follow you, if you hide
    The walls won't even ask you why.
    Miss Lonely, are you blue tonight?

Too tired for thoughts of suicide
You watch someone with eyelids wide
Some puppy who just takes it out of need
With life played out so violently
Cruel to the one watching wistfully
Never knowing to say help or to say please.

Oh, oh, come on, you can step inside,
The stairs won't follow you, if you hide
The walls won't even ask you why.
Miss Lonely, are you blue tonight?

IF I WERE A CARPENTER

Tim Hardin

If I were a carpenter
And you were a lady
Would you marry me anyway,
Would you have my baby?

If a tinker were my trade
Would you still love me?
Carrying the pots I made,
Following behind me.

> Save my love through loneliness,
> Save my love for sorrow.
> I've given you my ownliness
> Come and give me your tomorrow.

If I worked my hands in wood
Would you still love me?
Answer me, Baby, "Yes I would,
I'd put you above me."

If I were a miller
At a mill wheel grinding,
Would you miss your colored box,
Your soft shoes shining?

> Save my love through loneliness,
> Save my love for sorrow.
> I've given you my ownliness,
> Come and give me your tomorrow.

ALBATROSS

Judy Collins

The lady comes to the gate,
Dressed in lavender and leather
Looking north to the sea
She finds the weather fine,
She hears the steeple bells
Ringing through the orchard
All the way from town.
She watches sea gulls fly
Silver on the ocean
Stitching through the waves
The edges of the sky.

Many people wander up the hills
From all around you,
Making up your memories
And thinking they have found you,
They cover you with veils of wonder
As if you were a bride,
Young men holding violets
Are curious to know if you have cried,
And tell you why and ask you why,
Any way you answer.

Lace around the collars
Of the blouses of the ladies,
Flowers from a Spanish friend
Of the family,
The embroidery of your life
Holds you in and keeps you out

But you survive,
Imprisoned in your bones
Behind the isinglass windows
Of your eyes . . .

And in the night the iron wheels
rolling through the rain
Down the hills through the long grass
to the sea,
And in the dark the hard bells
ringing with pain
Come away alone . . .

Even now by the gate
With your long hair blowing,
And the colors of the day
That lie along your arms,
You must barter your life
To make sure you are living,
And the crowd that has come
You give them the colors,
And the bells and wind and the dreams.

Will there never be a prince
Who rides along the sea and the mountains,
Scattering the sand and foam
Into amethyst fountains,
Riding up the hills from the beach
In the long summer grass,
Holding the sun in his hands
And shattering the isinglass?

Day and night and day again,
And people come and go away forever,
While the shining summer sea
Dances in the glass of your mirror,

While you search the waves for love
And your visions for a sign,
The knot of tears around your throat
Is crystalizing into your design . . .

    And in the night the iron wheels
        rolling through the rain
Down the hills through the long grass
        to the sea,
And in the dark the hard bells
        ringing with pain,
Come away alone . . .
Come away alone . . . with me.

DRAGON SONG

Carl Oglesby

Out beyond the plains where dragons play the sight
Of dancing shadow kings has caught your eye tonight
The fine and distant song the dragon gives the wind
Will leave my simple dream behind where your begins

The phantom dragon spreads his great bleeding wings
Across the moon he glides and you have listened to him sing
And I am left below to guard your drunken pleasure ship
A sleepy watchman I, for abandoned things

The moving figures on your old Grecian screen
And naked dancers in an ocean rolling wild and green
And circling up the stairs with motions ever unforeseen
You make your secret sign, I disappear

Maybe once or twice a certain smile will come
And you'll remember then that I am here alone
But pity's not the game, and all I really want to say
Is I'd like to hunt with you again in the royal dragon way.

CHAPTER THREE

COMMUNITY

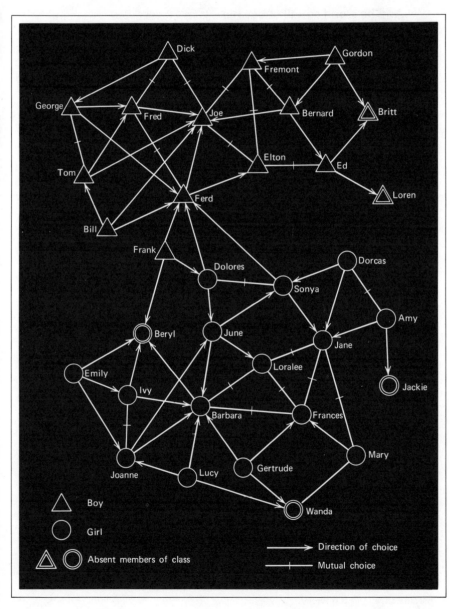

STORY OF ISAAC

Leonard Cohen

The door it opened slowly
   My father he came in
   I was nine years old
And he stood so tall above me
   Blue eyes they were shining
   And his voice was very cold.
Said, "I've had a vision
   And you know I'm strong and holy
   I must do what I've been told."
So he started up the mountain
   I was running he was walking
   And his ax was made of gold.

The trees they got much smaller
   The lake a lady's mirror
   We stopped to drink some wine
Then he threw the bottle over
   Broke a minute later
   And he put his hand on mine.
Thought I saw an eagle
   But it might have been a vulture,
   I never could decide.
Then my father built an altar
   He looked once behind his shoulder
   He knew I would not hide.

You who build the altars now
   To sacrifice these children
   You must not do it any more.

A scheme is not a vision
    And you never have been tempted
    By a demon or a god.
You who stand above them now
    Your hatchets blunt and bloody,
    You were not there before.
When I lay upon a mountain
    And my father's hand was trembling
    With the beauty of the word.

And if you call me brother now
    Forgive me if I inquire
    Just according to whose plan?
When it all comes down to dust
    I will kill you if I must
    I will help you if I can.
When it all comes down to dust
    I will help you if I must
    I will kill you if I can.
And mercy on our uniform
Man of peace or man of war-
    The peacock spreads his fan.

1. Read the biblical story of Isaac. What seems to you to be the point of the biblical story? Note Cohen's additions to the story: Why nine years old specifically? What is the significance of the door? (Semitic nomads lived in tents.) How many levels of meaning might be involved? Do blue eyes fit your ideas of semitic people? Would Abraham have had blue eyes? Is this detail significant in terms of the theme of the poem?

2. Does the juxtaposition of brother and war suggest any other biblical stories of brothers in conflict? In what way would these stories contribute to the theme of the poem?

3. Who is the speaker addressing when he says "you who build the altars now"? How many kinds of altars could these lines apply to?

4. Does the mention of uniforms necessarily limit your approach to this poem as merely a war protest poem? Could uniforms refer to love beads, the gray-flannel suit, skin color, etc.? In what sense do all of us wear uniforms?

5. What is the implication of the lines, "He knew I would not hide"? How does this relate to the situation of today's sacrificial children?

6. Consider the inversion of "I will kill you if I must/I will help you if I can" to "I will help you if I must/I will kill you if I can." What changes of meaning are suggested by these lines? Can you relate the lines to "fighting for peace"?

7. Why is the ax made of gold? How does this detail suggest an antithesis between the first two stanzas and the last two? List all the contrasting, antithetical images. In what sense is the poem built around the idea of antithesis? How do these contrasts contribute to theme?

8. What about that final image? How many things can it symbolize? How does it relate to the idea of uniforms as symbolic?

WHERE HAVE ALL THE FLOWERS GONE?

Peter Seeger

Where have all the flowers gone?
Long time passing
Where have all the flowers gone?
Long time ago
Where have all the flowers gone?
Young girls have picked them, every one.
Oh, when will they ever learn?
Oh, when will they ever learn?

Where have all the young girls gone?
Long time passing
Where have all the young girls gone?
Long time ago
Where have all the young girls gone?
They've taken husbands, every one.
Oh, when will they ever learn?
Oh, when will they ever learn?

Where have all the husbands gone?
Long time passing
Where have all the husbands gone?
Long time ago
Where have all the husbands gone?
Gone for soldiers, every one.
Oh, when will they ever learn?
Oh, when will they ever learn?

Where have all the soldiers gone?
Long time passing
Where have all the soldiers gone?
Long time ago

Where have all the soldiers gone?
Gone to graveyards, every one.
Oh, when will they ever learn?
Oh, when will they ever learn?

Where have all the graveyards gone?
Long time passing
Where have all the graveyards gone?
Long time ago
Where have all the graveyards gone?
They're covered with flowers, every one.
Oh, when will they ever learn?
Oh, when will they ever learn?

Where have all the flowers gone?
Long time passing
Where have all the flowers gone?
Long time ago
Where have all the flowers gone?
Young girls have picked them, every one.
Oh, when will they ever learn?
Oh, when will they ever learn?

1. The song ends where it had begun. Do you find this to be aesthetically pleasing? Can you think of any other songs (or any works of art) that have a cyclical structure? Is the form a message in itself?

2. flowers to girls to boys to soldiers to graveyards to flowers
           ashes to ashes and dust to dust
              and flowers to
                 flowers

   Is this a *natural* life cycle? What does the speaker want "them" to learn? Who are "they"?

3. Explore the symbolic implications of "flowers" in the poem's context.

4. "Incremental repetition" is a term coined by F. B. Gummere to describe a structural and/or rhetorical device peculiar to English and Scottish folk ballads (see Gummere, *The Popular Ballad,* 1904, 1907, especially pp. 117-124). The device is characterized by the repetition of a stanza (or sometimes a line) several times, but with key words changing in each stanza. How does incremental repetition work in this song? What effect does it have . . . on our ears? On the drama? On the message? Is the device especially suited to this song?

5. You might like to do some reading about the ballad and its tradition so you can consider this song in a broader context. Consult the reading list at the back of the book for some directions on where to begin. (Leslie Shepard's *The Broadside Ballad* provides fascinating material concerning types of ballads.)

6. What kind of a comment on war does the poem make? Is the treatment elliptical? (Are we to read-listen between the lines?)

7. The *ubi sunt* (where are . . .) motif has a long tradition in poetry, especially lyric poetry. Poems that were laments (or possibly ironic commentaries) listed names of people who were dead and gone, either heroes who had died in battle, or great rulers, or perhaps beautiful women. The Bible, with its long geneological lists, is a possible source for the tradition. *Ubi sunt* characteristically emphasizes the impermanence of life, or the degeneracy of an age. The motif enjoyed great vogue in the Middle Ages.

   Can we fit this poem in the *ubi sunt* tradition? Why are all verbs but one in the past tense? Does the poet leave us any hope?

8. At folk festivals, peace gatherings etc., this song probably vies with any other as the one that is most often sung by the entire assemblage. Why do you think this would be so? Could it have any relation to the concept of "chorus" that goes back to the Greeks?

THE CONTINUING STORY OF BUNGALOW BILL

John Lennon and Paul McCartney

Hey, Bungalow Bill
What did you kill
Bungalow Bill?

He went out tiger hunting with his elephant and gun.
In case of accidents he always took his mom.
He's the all American bullet-headed saxon mother's son.

All the children sing
Hey, Bungalow Bill
What did you kill
Bungalow Bill

Deep in the jungle where the mighty tiger lies
Bill and his elephants were taken by surprise.
So Captain Marvel zapped him right between the eyes.

All the children sing
Hey, Bungalow Bill
What did you kill
Bungalow Bill?

The children asked him if to kill was not a sin.
Not when he looked so fierce, his mother butted in.
If looks could kill it would have been us instead of him.

All the children sing
Hey, Bungalow Bill
What did you kill
Bungalow Bill?

1. Buffalo Bill was a historical figure about whom many legendary stories evolved, and these were adopted into the American frontier mythology. As e. e. cummings' poem tells us, "Buffalo Bill's defunct." Is Bungalow Bill a modern American reincarnation? Why is the poem called "The Continuing Story of . . ."? What other associations does "Bungalow" suggest?

2. How many implications can you derive from the epithet "All American bullet-headed saxon mother's son"?

3. Why is he hunting tigers? Why not buffalo? What relationships does this poem have with the two Buffy Sainte-Marie poems on pp. 69-73?

4. Captain Marvel is another mythical hero, but from the world of comic books. What is the function of his appearance on the scene?

5. Discuss the mother as stereotype. Is she an American stereotype? *Strictly* an American stereotype?

6. Examine the satiric function of the chorus. Why children, and why are they singing? What is the answer to the question they ask?

7. Is the satire directed solely at America?

8. Do you think that the poem's principal focus is on an antiwar and violence message?

9. When a poem is printed on a page (see page 64), does its configuration influence the reader's interpretation in *any* way? If so, do you think the influence varies from configuration to configuration, from poem to poem?

THE KLAN

David Arkin and Alan Arkin

The countryside was cold and still
There was a cross upon the hill
This cold cross wore a burning hood
To hide its rotten heart of wood.
Father, I hear the iron sound
Of hoofbeats on the frozen ground

Down from the hills the riders came,
Jesus, it was a crying shame
To see the blood upon their whips
And hear the snarling of their lips.
Mother, I feel a stabbing pain.
Blood flows down like a summer rain.

Now each one wore a mask of white
To hide his cruel face from sight,
And each one sucked a little breath
Out of the empty lungs of death.
Sister, lift my bloody head.
It's so lonesome to be dead.

He who travels with the Klan
Is a monster, not a man,
Underneath that white disguise
I have looked into his eyes.
Brother, will you stand with me?
It's not easy to be free.

1. Are you struck by the vivid imagery?
   Note the use of sounds:
   > "hoofbeats on the frozen ground"
   > "the snarling of their lips"
   > "sucked a hungry breath"

   Note the use of visual images:
   > blood, fire, hoods, whips

   Is this a surrealistic scene or a superrealistic scene?
   Note the movement from long shot to close up, as with a movie camera:
   > countryside cross burning hoods
   > riders coming downhill blood on whips

   The movement provides a visual effect much like montage in a film. Do the first three stanzas resemble a short sequence from a film?

2. Examine the following pairs of lines, and discuss the distinction between literal and figurative meaning:
   > Now each one wore a mask of white
   > To hide his cruel face from sight.
   > . . . .
   > And each one sucked a little breath
   > Out of the empty lungs of death.

   What figures are used in the second pair?

3. Note the contrast between the crystal clear physical imagery and the ambiguity of the narrator's experience. What effect does this have? Does the poem invite you to complete its story?

4. Discuss the possibility of an allusion to the horsemen of the Apocalypse. What contribution would this allusion make?

5. What can you say about the relationship between statement and image in this poem? Between statement and metaphor? Between statement and symbol?

6. Why does the speaker call out to every possible relationship in a family?

7. "It's not easy to be free." Whose freedom is the speaker referring to? Only his own? Examine the concept of freedom, as expressed and implied in this poem, and as applied to your own ideas about the relationship between the individual and his community.

FOR WHAT IT'S WORTH

Stephen Stills

There's something happenin' here.
What it is ain't exactly clear.
There's a man with a gun over there,
Tellin' me I've got to beware.
It's time we stop, children,
What's that sound?
Everybody look what's goin' down.

There's battle lines bein' drawn,
Nobody's right if everybody's wrong.
Young people speakin' their minds,
Gettin' so much resistance from behind.
It's time we stop, children,
What's that sound?
Everybody look what's goin' down.

What a field day for the heat.
A thousand people in the street,
Singin' songs and carryin' signs.
Mostly saying, "Hooray for our side."
It's time we stop, children,
What's that sound?
Everybody look what's goin' down.

Paranoia strikes deep,
Into your life it will creep.
It starts when you're always afraid,
Step out of line, the Man come
And take you away.
You better stop, hey,
What's that sound?
Everybody look what's goin' down.

1 . The colloquial language of this poem utilizes a number of slang expressions. Does the slang function as metaphor? Do you think the slang is appropriate to the "message" of the poem? Does it affect tone?

2. Notice the tension between "us" and "them." Is the speaker taking sides? Who is he speaking to? What is his message? What is "that sound"? What is "going down"?

3. "For What It's Worth"—how many things could "it" refer to? How many meanings could "worth" have?

4. "A thousand people in the street"
   "Hooray for our side."
   Does this constitute a community? If so, what kind?

NOW THAT THE BUFFALO'S GONE
Buffy Sainte-Marie

Can you remember the times
That you have held your head high
And told all your friends of your Indian claim
Proud good lady and proud good man
Your great great grandfather from Indian blood sprang
And you feel in your heart for these ones

Oh it's written in books and in songs
That we've been mistreated and wronged
Well over and over I hear the same words
From you good lady and you good man
But listen to me if you care where we stand
And you feel you're a part of these ones

When a war between nations is lost
The loser we know pays the cost
But even when Germany fell to your hands
Consider, dear lady, consider dear man
You left them their pride and you left them their lands
And what have you done to these ones?

Has a change come about Uncle Sam
Or are you still taking our lands?
A treaty forever George Washington signed
He did, dear lady, he did, dear man
And the treaty's being broken by Kinzua Dam
And what will you do for these ones?

Oh it's all in the past you can say
But it's still going on here today
The government now wants the Iroquois land
That of the Seneca and the Cheyenne
It's here and it's now you must help us dear man
Now that the buffalo's gone.

1. To whom is the poem addressed?

2. Can you identify tone? What is the attitude of the speaker towards the subject? Towards the person(s) addressed? (How did you go about finding your answers?)

3. What is the effect of addressing the country directly as "Uncle Sam"? Also, why do you think Washington is named directly, and why is the Kinzua Dam specifically mentioned?

4. Identify the specific kinds of end rhymes used in the poem. Do they have a particular function?

5. "Now that the buffalo's gone": consider the strategic placement of the line. How important is the line to the poem? Does it make a statement, or is it merely an allusion? Is the buffalo a symbol in American culture? If so, does its symbolization change within the poem's context?

MY COUNTRY 'TIS OF THY PEOPLE YOU'RE DYING
Buffy Sainte-Marie

Now that your big eyes have finally opened
Now that you're wondering how must they feel
Meaning them that you've chased across America's movie screens
Now that you're wondering how can it be real
That the ones you've called colorful, noble and proud
In your school propaganda
They starve in their splendor
You've asked for my comment I simply will render

My country 'tis of thy people you're dying.

Now that the long houses breed superstition
You force us to send our toddlers away
To your schools where they're taught to despise their
     traditions
You forbid them their languages then further say
That American history really began
When Columbus set sail out of Europe, then stress
That the nation of leeches that's conquered this land
Are the biggest and bravest and boldest and best
And yet where in your history books is the tale
Of the genocide basic to this country's birth
Of the preachers who lied, how the bill of rights failed
How a nation of patriots returned to their earth
And where will it tell of the liberty bell
As it rang with a thud
O'er Kinzua mud
And of brave Uncle Sam in Alaska this year

My country 'tis of thy people you're dying.

Hear how the bargain was made for the West
With her shivering children in zero degrees
Blankets for your land so the treaties attest
Oh well blankets for land is a bargain indeed
And the blankets were those Uncle Sam had collected
From smallpox-diseased dying soldiers that day
And the tribes were wiped out and the history books censored
A hundred years of your statesmen have felt it's better
        this way
And yet a few of the conquered have somehow survived
Their blood runs the redder though genes have paled
From the grand canyon's caverns to craven sad hills
The wounded, the losers, the robbed sing their tale
From Los Angeles County to upstate New York
The white nation fattens while others grow lean
Oh the tricked and evicted they know what I mean

My country 'tis of thy people you're dying.

The past it just crumbled the future just threatens
Our life blood shot up in your chemical tanks
And now here you come bill of sale in your hand
And surprise in your eyes that we're lacking in thanks
For the blessings of civilization you've brought us
The lessons you've taught us the ruin you've wrought us
Oh see what our trust in America's brought us

My country 'tis of thy people you're dying.

Now that the pride of the sires receives charity
Now that we're harmless and safe behind laws
Now that my life's to be known as your "heritage"
Now that even the graves have been robbed
Now that our own chosen way is a novelty
Hands on our hearts we salute you your victory

Choke on your blue white and scarlet hypocrisy
Pitying the blindness that you've never seen
That the eagles of war whose wings lent you glory
They were never no more than carrion crows
Pushed the wrens from their nest, stole their eggs, changed
    their story
The mockingbird sings it, it's all that he knows
"Ah what can I do," say a powerless few
With a lump in your throat and a tear in your eye
Can't you see that their poverty's profiting you

My country 'tis of thy people you're dying.

My country 'tis of thee
Sweet land of liberty
Of thee I sing.

1. Examine the change in tone between this poem and the preceding, "Now That the Buffalo's Gone." Which do you think is more effective? (Can such a comparison be made?) Who is being addressed in this poem?

2. Which lines insure the poem's topicality? Is topicality good or bad? Was your answer to the last question based on aesthetic considerations?

3. Probe the structure and the implications of the one-line refrain "My country 'tis of thy people you're dying."

4. "Now That the Buffalo's Gone" is a pure statement, except for its last line, which incorporates a symbol and profoundly affects the song. What role does figurative language play in the total experience of "My Country 'Tis of Thy People You're Dying"?

5. When Buffy Sainte-Marie sings these two songs, what does the emotion projected in her voice add to them? In particular, how does it affect "tone"?

6. Discuss the validity of the kinds of accusations made in this poem. Do you think their validity differs from the specific to the general? To separate myth from history and aid in your discussion, consult the list of suggested readings for information about the history of Indians and the situation of Indians today:

Vine Deloria, Jr. *Custer Died for Your Sins.* 1969.
Hal Borland. *When the Legends Die.* 1963.
Thomas Berger. *Little Big Man.* 1964.
Dan Cushman. *Stay Away, Joe.* 1953.
William T. Hagan. *American Indians.* 1961.
Angie Debo. *The Road to Disappearance.* 1941.
Ralph K. Andrist. *The Long Death.* 1964.
Alvin M. Josephy, Jr. *The Indian Heritage of America.* 1968.

TIN CAN ALLEY

Eric Andersen

Cop is on the corner lookin' down the street
Lookin' for the runner who's comin' with a treat
Crime, it don't exist if you look the other way
'Cause it's only in the movies when it never pays
To get you in the jail house the cops they got their tricks
You don't fight back son unless you're lookin' to get hit
In Tin Can Alley the cops they get their kicks
'Cause they know who it is a-carryin' the sticks.

Hallway nightmares blacken out the moon
Someone's on the landing just fumbled with the spoon,
Stay for awhile, but you can't stay here
'Cause the man is a-comin' and he might be near.
He knows you'll come lookin' if you don't get some
He follows like a vulture till your mind's undone,
You're crazy like a rat but you just don't run
Down in Tin Can Alley with your back to the sun.

Shoebox halls ain't very much space,
It ain't just kids that overrun the place.
Rats in cupboard papa just sighs
Mama is afraid they'll make the baby cry.
They creep along the ceilings; they creep along the walls,
Landlord's out every time you call.
You're so scared at night you can't walk out in the halls
'Cause down Tin Can Alley they ain't afraid of you at all.

Outdoor sun gives a kid a clean mind,
But there ain't no trees, just some old street signs.

Ain't no place to run and fall,
So you learn how to box your shadow on the wall.
Smokestack's coughin' a couple blocks away,
The air's so dirty, the sheets are turning gray,
It looks like midnight, it's the middle of the day
Down in Tin Can Alley where the little kids play.

Church is on the corner inheriting the poor
While the earth is in a vault locked inside the door.
Repent and it is yours the promise that they give,
And you hope and pray that Jesus can remember where you live.
Oh, you were born to suffer the preacher he believes
Pay for all your sins now and get down on your knees.
You've been down so long that you don't know what it means
Or why parked out in the alley is a chauffeured limousine.

There's a hungry politician tryin' to win your vote,
Kissin' all the babies to fill you full of hope,
He promises you everything, he promises you the sun
He tells you to believe the battle could be won,
But after he's elected and the race is run
He never comes around, he must be dumb.
While all the racketeers are throwin' sugar on his tongue
Down in Tin Can Alley where nothin's ever done.

Mama's little angel didn't mean to go wrong,
When daddy disappeared another came along,
Start out in the streets to find a good time,
To end up on the roof for a nickel and a dime.
You really can't believe this is happening to you.
Then a couple mouths to feed and no money comin' through,
But hustlin' up the rent can be an easy thing to do,
'Cause down in Tin Can Alley mama had to do it too.

There's a junkyard poet sniffin' all around,
His ear up to the radio to hear what's goin' down.
He gets Tin Pan Sally and Little Boy Blue
Singin' all about the things that never come true
While back in the shadows his songs are sung
To a tin can band on a tin can drum
On a tin can line his words are strung
With an eye on the pencil and a hand on the gun.

1. How do images of animals and darkness express the theme of the poem?

2. The common cliché is "he promises you the moon." Why, in this poem, does the speaker say "he promises you the sun"?

3. What is the effect of the repetition of "tin can"? How does this relate to theme?

4. Note the "tin can" slang and cliché language of the poem. (How) does the language contribute to the force of the poem? Compare the language use with songs like "For What It's Worth," "How Long," and "Spoonful."

5. Is there an affirmation in the poem? If there is, what is its nature?

STORIES OF THE STREET
Leonard Cohen

The stories of the street are mine
The Spanish voices laugh
The Cadillacs go creeping down
Through the night and the poison gas.
I lean from my window sill
In this old hotel I chose
One hand on my suicide
One hand on the rose.

I know you've heard it's over now
And war must surely come
The cities they are broke in half
And the middle men are gone.
But let me ask you one more time
O, children of the dust,
All these hunters who are shrieking now
Do they speak for us?

And where do all these highways go
Now that we are free?
Why are the armies marching still
That were coming home to me?
O, lady with your legs so fine
O, stranger at your wheel
You are locked into your suffering
And your pleasures are the seal

The age of lust is giving birth
And both the parents ask
The nurse to tell them fairy tales
On both sides of the glass
Now the infant with his cord
Is hauled in like a kite
And one eye filled with blueprints
One eye filled with night.

O, come with me my little one
And we will find that farm
And grow us grass and apples there
And keep all the animals warm.
And if by chance I wake at night
And I ask you who I am
O, take me to the slaughter house
I will wait there with the lamb.

With one hand on a hexagram
And one hand on a girl
I balance on a wishing well
That all men call the world.
We are so small between the stars
So large against the sky
And lost among the subway crowds
I try to catch your eye.

1. Each stanza of the poem presents a kind of vignette, a "story of the street."
   What is the subject of each story? Consider specific images in each stanza:
   Why "Spanish" voices?
   Who are the middle men who are gone?
   Who are the hunters?
   Why are pleasures the seal of suffering?
   What is the implication of "one eye filled
      with blueprints/One eye filled with night"?
   Why do the parents want to hear "fairy tales"?
   What is the allusion in the reference to the
      slaughter house and the lamb? Does "The
      Butcher," by Leonard Cohen suggest an answer?
   What sources of refuge are suggested in the
      first pair of lines in the final stanza?
   Why is the world described as a wishing well?

2. What allusion to biblical myths can you find in the poem? What is their significance?

3. Now consider the poem as a whole. Does the poem mention every major problem of our twentieth-century world? Or are some missing? Is there any affirmation or optimism in the poem?

4. How many images can you find in the poem that imply that the speaker is demanding that his audience make a choice? How many choices are there? Does the poem supply a "blueprint" toward a way out of the dilemma it presents?

THE GATES OF EDEN
Bob Dylan

Of war and peace the truth just twists
Its curfew gull it glides
Upon four legged forest clouds
The cowboy angel rides
With his candle lit into the sun
Though its glow is waxed in black
All except when 'neath the trees of Eden.

2.

The lamp post stands with folded arms
Its iron claws attached
To curbs 'neath holes where babies wail
Though it shadows metal badge
All in all can only fall
With a crashing but meaningless blow
No sound ever comes from The Gates of Eden.

3.

This savage soldier sticks his head in sand
And then complains
Unto the shoeless hunter who's gone deaf
But still remains
Upon the beach where hound dogs bay
At ships with tattooed sails
Heading for The Gates of Eden.

4.

With a time rusted compass blade
Aladdin and his lamp
Sits with Utopian hermit monks
Side saddle on the Golden Calf

And on their promises of paradise
You will not hear a laugh
All except inside The Gates of Eden.

5.

Relationships of ownership
They whisper in the wings
To those condemned to act accordingly
And wait for succeeding kings
And I try to harmonize with songs
The lonesome sparrow sings
There are no kings inside The Gates of Eden.

6.

The motorcycle black madonna
Two wheeled gypsy queen
And her silver studded phantom cause
The grey flannel dwarf to scream
As he weeps to wicked birds of prey
Who pick up on his bread crumb sins
And there are no sins inside The Gates of Eden.

7.

The Kingdoms of experience
In the precious winds they rot
While paupers change possessions
Each one wishing for what the other has got
And the princess and the prince
Discuss what's real and what is not
It doesn't matter inside The Gates of Eden.

8.

The foreign sun it squints upon
A bed that is never mine
As friends and other strangers
From their fates try to resign

Leaving men holy totally free
To do anything they wish to do but die
And there are no trials inside The Gates of Eden.

9.

At dawn my lover comes to me
And tells me of her dreams
With no attempts to shovel a glimpse
Into the ditch of what each one means
At times I think there are no words
But these to tell what's true
And there are no truths outside The Gates of Eden.

"A poem should not mean but be"
Archibald MacLeish

1. Copy the entire first stanza out in a single line. Now, punctuate it, using
   pause marks and end marks to separate what you consider to be units of
   meaning. Are your choices arbitrary? Can some phrases (or words) fit either
   with what precedes them or with what follows them? Do some units overlap?
   If so, what effect does this have on any attempts to derive "linear" meaning
   from the stanza?

2. Now consider the first stanza in relation to what follows. After thwarting our
   attempts to pigeonhole meaning (if you agree it does so), on what kind of a
   journey does the poem take us? In the final stanza, the speaker says his lover
   tells him of her unedited and uninterpreted dreams. How is the meaning of
   something a "ditch"? Can we relate the concept of "dream" to the structure
   of the poem? Does the term "surrealism" apply here? Can we see each
   succeeding stanza as a little tableau, a fragmented scene which flows through
   the stream of the unconscious, or the liberated consciousness?

3. In *The Mechanical Bride,* Marshall McLuhan said of Picasso: "He reduces a
   full length novel (or movie) like *Madame Bovary* to a single image of great
   intensity." Can such a comment be applied to Dylan in this poem? List the

things that are outside the Gates of Eden and things that are inside. Explore all the symbolic implications of "Gates of Eden."

4. The poem begins with a denial of truth and closes with a denial of truth, yet *is* a search for truth. Paradox? Find the specific paradox being used as a device in the last stanza. Is paradox an especially suitable form of expression in this poem?

5. How many different topics are being treated? Is the concern primarily social, metaphysical, or epistemological?

6. Discuss evidences of symbolism, metaphor, irony, allusion and allegory found within each stanza. Concentrate on one stanza, and extract, if you can, layers of "meaning."

   In stanza four, what does the laughter allude to? Could it be an allusion to Greek mythology?

NOBODY'S BUYING FLOWERS FROM THE FLOWER LADY
Phil Ochs

Millionaires and paupers walk the lonely street
Rich and poor companions of the restless feet
Strangers in a foreign land strike a match with a tremblin' hand
Learned too much to ever understand
But nobody's buying flowers from the flower lady.

Lovers quarrel, snarl away their happiness
Kisses crumble in a web of loneliness
It's written by the poison pen, voices break before they bend
The door is slammed, it's over once again
But nobody's buying flowers from the flower lady.

Poets agonize, they cannot find the words
The stone stares at the sculptor, asks are you absurd
The painter paints his brushes black, through the canvas
    runs a crack
The portrait of the pain never answers back
But nobody's buying flowers from the flower lady.

Soldiers disillusioned come home from the war
Sarcastic students tell them not to fight no more
And they argue through the night, black is black
    and white is white
Walk away both knowing they are right
Still nobody's buying flowers from the flower lady.

Smoke dreams of escaping soul are drifting by
Dull the pain of living as they slowly die
Smiles change into a sneer, washed away by whiskey tears
In the quicksand of their minds they disappear
But nobody's buying flowers from the flower lady.

Feeble aged people almost to their knees
Complain about the present using memories
Never found their pot of gold, wrinkled hands pound
    weary holes
Each line screams out you're old, you're old, you're old
But nobody's buying flowers from the flower lady.

And the flower lady hobbles home without a sale
Tattered shred of petals leave a fading trail
Not a pause to hold a rose, even she no longer knows
The lamp goes out, the evening now is closed
And nobody's buying flowers from the flower lady.

1. Can you categorize each stanza with regard to the particular aspect of society it portrays? Can you think of other social aspects that the poet could have included in the same scheme? From the topical choices he made, how would you say the poet views the concept of community?

2. What is the unifying agent between millionaires and paupers?

3. Is the phrase "Strangers in a foreign land" to be interpreted literally or metaphorically? Who are the strangers?

4. What are the quarreling lovers compared with through imagery?

5. In the third stanza, is the term "absurd" open to multiple interpretation?

6. How is the color of the painter's brushes symbolic? Compare with Mick Jagger's "Paint It Black."

7. What relationship is suggested between the artist and his art?

8. Is the fourth stanza about war or righteousness? How are the two concepts correlated?

9. In the fifth stanza, what feeling is communicated by the images alone?

10. What comment on old age does the sixth stanza make? How is this stanza prepared for thematically by the others?

11. Which is the image against which all the other aspects of society are contrasted—the flowers or the flower lady?

12. Compare the poem's theme and structure with Bob Dylan's "Gates of Eden" and Leonard Cohen's "Stories of the Street."

ALL ALONG THE WATCHTOWER
Bob Dylan

"There must be some way out of here,"
said the joker to the thief.
"There's too much confusion,
I can't get no relief."

"Bus'nessmen, they drink my wine,
plowmen dig my earth;
none of them along the line
know what any of it is worth."

"No reason to get excited,"
the thief he kindly spoke.
"There are many here among us
who feel that life is but a joke."

"But, you and I, we've been thru that,
and this is not our fate;
so, let us not talk falsely now,
the hour is getting late."

All along the watchtower,
princes kept the view,
while all the women came and went,
barefoot servants, too.

Outside in the distance,
a wildcat did growl.
Two riders were approaching.
The wind began to howl.

1 . Can you establish the setting? Does the watchtower sit upon the walls of a castle? A city? A prison? Is the time Medieval? Modern? What effects does the setting have on the total meaning of the poem?

2. joker
thief
businessmen
plowmen
princes
women
barefoot servants
Do the above constitute a community? If so, what kind?

3. Note all the ironic reversals. How do these figures and their situations clash with our typical (or stereotypical) conceptions of them? What do you think is the idea behind such reversals?

4. How many omens can you find? Are they good or evil omens? Do you get the feeling that whatever is going to happen, it will have a cataclysmic effect on this "community"?

PORTRAIT OF A LADY

Carl Oglesby

Soft rosy mist of dawn
Springtime in the country
She finds initials carved in stone
Of which she has some dim memory

Abandoned in her playground she arranges her toys
Trying to find a little peace of mind
She scavenges her scrapbook for snapshots of joy
Porcelain moments, simple and fine
The bombs are falling in the city once again
The light is growing vague
But the cries of pain are far away
And never could you say she'd ever closed her door

So she wonders why she feels ashamed
And why her kisses fade
And she wonders why there is no place to die to but the grave
And she's afraid
But she may wonder just what victories she can prize
Or faces that she'll recognize to praise

High, hot summer noon
Silver airplane crashes
East of her in a burning land
Each initial flashes

With a teacup in the garden or wading in the cove
Nice conversations flicker in her mind

Sundays with the family, a distant radio
Days of roses, nights of wine
A lavender or burning sky, the silhouettes of birds
Ah but now it seems absurd
That so easily she'd say she's satisfied
And just go gliding down as if she'd never tried to fly

Oh the heroes are so graceful
And the heroes are so pure
The broken faces in the papers tell her she's secure
But she's afraid
For still she wonders if the story's really through
Or if surviving's really what she's tried to do.

Pearl shadows in the church
A rainy dusk in fall
She finds initials in the dust
Whose however she cannot now recall

How fine her fingers at the spinet, how composed
A life's confessions summed up in a single tear
A cameo in bridal white, how pale in mourning gown
The gentle curse was mistaken for the prayer
Ah but all in all the picture's not much worse that it has been
And to say that it's all at its end
Is to see how very little she had cared
A thought she'd never dared at all to comprehend

So she summons up her courage
And she puts her hair in curls
And so prepares a face to face the mirror in the world
She's not afraid
For when surviving's not the thing you really want to do
Then nothing will seem very false or very true

Cat-ice forming on the brook
A silvery night in winter
She finds initials in the snow
Whose she can't remember
Perhaps she never really knew
Perhaps one day she'd better know
Perhaps one day she'll need to know

1. Compare Oglesby's portrait technique with that of Donovan in "Widow with Shawl." Can you visualize Oglesby's lady? On what do you base your impressions of her?

2. On the literal level, the poem paints a portrait of a lady. Can you detect other levels? Could the lady be a personification? Can you relate this lady to the virgin in "Suburbs of Eden"?

3. Notice the emphasis on settings. What kind of environment and way of life does the poet suggest through setting? Are any of the settings archetypal?

4. Find all the references to initials in the poem. Why has she forgotten whose they are? Why, do you think, that "one day she'll need to know" whose they are? Are the initials symbolic? Do you think they are all the same initials?

5. Note the poet's preoccupation with light. Does light have thematic or symbolic significance? For instance, does the reference to "a lavender or burning sky" mean more than simply two ways of describing the sky at sunset?

6. The poem carefully links the cycle of the seasons (spring, summer, fall, winter) with the cycle of the day (dawn, noon, dusk, night). Does this cycle have symbolic significance?

SUBURBS OF EDEN

Carl Oglesby

You may remember my surprise
When right before my eyes
You abandoned your disguise
Revealing to me
That you were not the little virgin
I had thought, you were the surgeon
Poised, knife in hand,
To deliver another little man

In the suburbs of Eden
The far outskirts of Paradise
Over yonder

The sky was silver at the end
You were reluctant to defend
The silence of your friend
Who didn't want to let me come back in
You hid your sin, I hid my crime
We drank a toast in local wine
Then we listened to the chimes of Easter morning

In the suburbs of Eden
The wild outskirts of Paradise
Over yonder

And now the virgin's in her coffin
In her gay chantilly gown
And the priests are shooting Paradise
In the meadows outside town

And yes she lies in state at Macy's
That's on the first floor mezzanine
You can buy your souvenir virgin there
Pull her wire, hear her scream

In the suburbs of Eden
The gay outskirts of Paradise
Over yonder

1. Go through the poem as the story of the relationship between two people.
   Characterize the girl and what has happened between them to bring them to
   this point. What is the significance of the refrain in this context?

2. Go through the poem on another level; consider the girl a personification of
   the country, the theme as social protest. What does the poem say about
   society? What are the implications of "shooting paradise" in this context?
   Could the line have several interpretations? What is the significance of the
   refrain in this context?

3. Consider the poem on still another level, with the girl a personification of
   religion, the theme as estrangement between man and God. What are the
   implications of "priests shooting paradise" now? Who are the priests? What is
   the significance of the refrain now?

4. Which interpretation do you think best fits the poem? Is it necessary to
   choose one? Can you propose another?

5. Notice the deterioration of the rhyme scheme as the poem progresses. Does
   this have a thematic significance?

TWELVE THIRTY
(YOUNG GIRLS ARE COMING TO THE CANYON)
John Phillips

I used to live in New York City
Everything there was dark and dirty
Outside my window was a steeple
With a clock that always said twelve thirty.

Young girls are coming to the canyon
And in the mornings I can see them walking
I can no longer keep my blinds drawn
And I can't keep myself from talking.

At first so strange to feel so friendly
To say good morning and really mean it
To feel these changes happening in me
But not to notice till I feel it

Young girls are coming to the canyon
And in the morning I can see them walking
I can no longer keep my blinds drawn
And I can't keep myself from talking.

Cloudy waters cast no reflection
Images of beauty lie there stagnant
Vibrations bounce in no direction
And lie there shattering into fragments.

Young girls are coming to the canyon
And in the morning I can see them walking
I can no longer keep my blinds drawn
And I can't keep myself from talking.

1. Discuss the implications of the title and the refrain. In the title, is the time of day significant? What time of day is it in the poem? Is it possible that the poem actually has two different titles?

2. What is the canyon the speaker refers to? If he *used to* live in New York City, then the implication is that the canyon is some place away from the "dark and dirty" city. But could the canyon *still* refer to the city?

   This brings up the problem of escape. Has the speaker of the poem actually left the city, or is the opening line a metaphorical expression of escape? Do verb tenses in the poem affect the answer to this question?

   In Book I of *Paradise Lost,* Satan, after having been hurled into hell, and after having recovered and regrouped his band of fallen angels, says in answer to their complaints about their situation:

   > The mind is its own place, and in itself
   > Can make a Heav'n of Hell, A Hell of Heav'n.

   Could the speaker in "Twelve Thirty" have chosen to make a heaven out of hell?

3. Compare the rhythm of the fifth stanza with that of the others. What do you think is the purpose of the uneven quality? The stanza deals with "images of beauty" that don't materialize. Besides "cloudy waters" are there any other images at all within the stanza itself? Could the medium be the message?

ATLANTIS

Donovan Leitch

The continent of Atlantis was an island which lay before the great flood in the area we now call the Atlantic Ocean. So great an area of land, that from her western shores, those beautiful sailors journeyed to the south and the North Americas with ease, in their ships with painted sails. To the east Africa was a neighbor across a short strait of sea miles. The great Egyptian age is but a remnant of the Atlantian culture. The antedeluvian Kings colonized—All the Gods who play in the mythological dramas in all legends from all lands were from fair Atlantis. Knowing her fate, Atlantis sent out ships to all corners of the earth—On board were the twelve, the poet, the physician, the farmer, the scientist, the magician, and the other so called Gods of our legends—Tho' Gods they were and as the elders of our time choose to remain blind, let us rejoice and let us sing and dance and ring in the new. Hail Atlantis!

Way down—below the ocean—were I wanna be—she may be

ATLANTIS

Donovan Leitch

The continent of Atlantis
Was an island
Which lay before the great flood
In the area we now call
The Atlantic Ocean.

So great an area of land,
That from her western shores,
Those beautiful sailors
Journeyed to the south and the North Americas
with ease,
In their ships with painted sails.

To the east Africa was a neighbor
Across a short strait of sea miles.
The great Egyptian age is but a remnant
Of the Atlantian culture.

The antedeluvian Kings colonized—
All the Gods who play
In all legends
From all lands
Were from fair Atlantis.

Knowing her fate,
Atlantis sent out ships
To all corners of the earth—
On board were
the twelve,
the poet,
the physician,

the farmer,
the scientist,
the magician,
and the other so called
Gods of our legends—

Tho Gods they were

And as the elders of our time
Choose to remain blind,
Let us rejoice
And let us sing
And dance
And ring in the new.

Hail Atlantis!

Way down
Below the ocean
Where I wanna be
She may be

1. How would you characterize the tone of the poem? Consider the ambiguity of the section, "As the elders of our time choose to remain blind . . . let us rejoice . . . " Are the elders of our time blind to our impending fate, or to the fact that we are the children of gods? Is the poem a celebration of our divinity, or a lament for the fate that awaits us?

2. You might want to do some reading about the legend of Atlantis. (Plato's *Timaeus* and *Critias* describe the lost community and hint at the reasons for its fall.) Donovan's poem specifically connects Atlantis with our own society. What relationship can you find between the myth of Atlantis and contemporary society? Has Donovan changed or added to the myth? What effect, if any, does his treatment of the myth have on your interpretation of the poem?

3. What is the significance of the catalog of the survivors of Atlantis? Notice that the list begins "the twelve" and continues with specific titles—"the poet," "the physician," etc. Do you detect any ambiguity? Are "the twelve" another category? Does it matter? Does "the twelve" suggest any allusions outside the Atlantis myth? If so, is this important?

   Notice that there is no priest in the group. Does this strike you as significant? Are there any others listed who might fulfill a priestly function?

   If a recording is available, listen to the song before you go on to the next question.

4. Now, what is the effect of the prolonged repetition of the final lines? What were you thinking of when the song ended? Compare your answer with others in the class.

5. a. The greatest number of words in "Atlantis" are spoken rather than sung. Could the first part be a prologue? An introduction? An extended title? Can there be a song without a singer? What constitutes a song?
   b. "Atlantis" normally appears in print arranged as prose. Compare the prose version with the version following it which is arranged in poetic stanzas. Does this arrangement make it a poem? Or was it a poem anyway? What constitutes a poem?

THE END

Jim Morrison

This is the end,
Beautiful friend,
This is the end,
My only friend,
The end of our elaborate plans,
The end of everything that stands,
The end. No safety or surprise,
The end. I'll never look into your eyes
Again.

Can you picture what will be
So limitless and free,
Desperately in need of some stranger's hand
In a desperate land.
Lost in a Roman wilderness of pain
And all the children are insane;
Waiting for the summer rain.

There's danger on the edge of town,
Ride the king's highway.
Weird scenes inside the gold mine;
Ride the king's highway west, baby.
Ride the snake
To the lake
The ancient lake.
The snake is long
Seven miles;
Ride the snake,
He's old and his skin is cold.

The West is the best.
The West is the best.
Get here and we'll do the rest.
The blue bus is calling us.
Driver, where are you taking us?

The killer awoke before dawn,
He puts his boots on,
He took a face from the ancient gallery,
And he walked on down the hall.
He went to the room where his sister lived,
And then he paid a visit to his brother,
And then he walked on down the hall.
And he came to a door.
And he looked inside
"Father?"
"Yes, son?"
"I want to kill you."
"Mother, I want . . . "

Come on baby, take a chance with us,
And meet me by the back of the blue bus.

This is the end,
Beautiful friend.
This is the end,
My only friend, the end.
It hurts to set you free
But you'll never follow me
The end of laughter and soft lies,
The end of night we tried to die.
This is the end.

1. Discuss images or aspects of sexual obsession, of violation, of insanity (personal and social). What is the relationship between sexual obsession and insanity in the poem? Is it possible to determine whether one is the cause of the other? Is it possible to determine whether one is dominant?

2. What is the relationship between the spoken section (the italicized portion of the poem) and the rest of the poem? Could this section be a dramatization of what is going on in the rest of the poem?

3. Find the Oedipus allusion and discuss its relationship to the rest of the poem. Does it shed any light on the problems raised by questions one and two?

4. Notice the metamorphoses in the poem: the highway, the bus, the snake, the hall. Do they connect with sexual obsession? With insanity? With the allusion to Oedipus?

BLACK PANTHER

Carl Oglesby

I warned you things were crumbling
You could feel the storm in the air
You just showed me your Japanese umbrella
So cool, so debonair

Icecubes tinkled
The conversation strayed
To cocktail observations
On the one who was trying to pray

I cried in the name of your Jesus
Beware the big-time brass
You just stood there with your lollipop eyes
Like stoned on a kilo of grass

Oh the panther with the burning wound
Has found your perfume trail
You sit there tolling your I*Ching changes
And you won't even open your special-delivery mail

Oh the panther gonna get your mama
Oh the panther gonna love your lamb
Spaced out of your mind on your dime horoscope
You got the virgin going down on the ram

Don't you know your garden is weedy
Don't you know your vineyards are bare
Dry well, poison water,
And your stallion is eating your mare

Well footman, footman, better shut the gates
Make sure the windows are closed

I told you baby that was just not enough
You just sat in your swing sniffing your rose

Footman, footman, better bring his coach
Better bring round this young man's cape
Seems to me it's about time he should leave
He's had a bit much of that old vino veritas grape

But the footman, he just stands there
Just looks you cold up and down
So you tell him, Boy, don't get insolent
And you try not to notice his frown

Then you feel yourself growing weary
And you hear a strange breathing at your side
Well maybe you better hurry up baby
Better find yourself some place to hide

Then the trees, they turn into husbands
The roses turn into wives
The night comes down, it's black panther town
The children turn into knives

Well, I warned you in the morning
You would never make high noon
You just swivled around like some satisfied woman
Crooning your personal tunes

But now that your fine lips are bleeding
And you burn from a thousand rapes
And your bare body is learning
The name of the game and the stakes

You'll remember the way back to human
You'll remember the way back to soul
You'll remember the way it all come down
You'll pick up your ruins and go down one more road

BLACK PANTHER

Carl Oglesby

I told you things were crumbling
You could smell the storm in the air
You just showed me your Japanese umbrella
So cool, so debonair

Ice cubes tinkled
The conversation strayed
To cocktail party observations
On the one who was trying to pray

I told you in the name of your Jesus
You better beware the big time brass
You just stood there with your lollipop eyes
Like stoned on a kilo of grass

Well, the panther with the burning wound
Has found your perfume trail
You stand there roving your I Ching changes
And you won't even open up your special delivery mail

Yea, the panther gonna get your mama
Panther gonna get your lamb
You stand there with your dime horoscope
You got the Virgo down on the Ram

You know your garden is weedy
Don't you know your vineyard is bare
Dry well, poison water
Your stallion is eating your mare

Well, footman, footman, shut the gates
Make sure the windows are closed
I told you baby that was just not enough
You just sat there in your swing sniffing your rose

Well, footman, footman, bring his coach
Footman, better bring this young man's cape
Seems to me it's about time for him to leave
Yes, he's had a bit much of that old vino veritas grape

Ah, but the footman he just stands there
He just looks you up and down
You tell him, "Boy, don't get insolent"
And you try not to notice his frown

And you feel yourself growing weary
And you hear strange breathing at your side
And maybe you better hurry up baby
Better find yourself a place to hide

And then the trees turn into husbands
And the roses turn into wives
And the night goes down to panther town
And the children turn into knives

Well, I warned you in the morning
You would never make high noon
You just stood there like some satisfied woman
Involved in your personal tunes

Well, now that your fine lips are bleeding
And you burn from a thousand rapes
Yes, and your bare body is learn-learn-learning
The name of the game and the stakes

You'll remember the way back to human
You'll remember the way back to soul
You'll remember the way it all come down
You'll pick up your ruins and go down one more road

Pick up your ruins and go down one more road . . .

1. Compare the two versions of this poem. The first is taken from the written lyrics; the second is a voice transcription of the song as recorded by Carl Oglesby. Go through the two poems carefully, noting the changes in the recorded version. Which version do you like better? Do the changes improve the poem's "literary" qualities? Do the changes affect your response to the poem? If at all possible, listen to Oglesby sing this song. Now consider the comments in Chapter I on the relationships between music, song, and poetry. Refer to Ginsberg's remarks about poetry "invoked shamanistically on the spot from the unconscious." Do these comments help to explain the phenomenon of this song?

THE SOUND OF SILENCE
Paul Simon

Hello darkness my old friend,
I've come to talk with you again,
Because a vision softly creeping,
Left its seeds while I was sleeping
And the vision that was planted in my brain
Still remains within the sound of silence.

In restless dreams I walked alone,
Narrow streets of cobble stone
'Neath the halo of a street lamp,
I turned my collar to the cold and damp
When my eyes were stabbed by the flash of a neon light
That split the night, and touched the sound of silence.

And in the naked light I saw
Ten thousand people maybe more,
People talking without speaking,
People hearing without listening,
People writing songs that voices never share
And no one dares disturb the sound of silence.

"Fools!" said I, "You do not know
Silence like a cancer grows.
Hear my words that I might teach you
Take my arms that I might reach you."
But my words like silent raindrops fell
And echoed, in the wells of silence.

And the people bowed and prayed
To the neon God they made,
And the sign flashed out its warning
In the words that it was forming.
And the sign said:
    "The words of the prophets are written
    on the subway walls and tenement halls"
And whispered in the sound of silence.

PENNY LANE

John Lennon and Paul McCartney

In Penny Lane there is a barber showing photographs
of ev'ry head he's had the pleasure to know
And all the people that come and go
stop and say "Hello."

On the corner is a banker with a motorcar,
the little children laugh at him behind his back
And the banker never wears a mac
In the pouring rain—
very strange.

Penny Lane is in my ears and in my eyes,
there beneath the blue suburban skies
I sit, and meanwhile back

In Penny Lane there is a fireman with an hourglass
and in his pocket is a portrait of the Queen.
He likes to keep his fire engine clean,
it's a clean machine.

Penny Lane is in my ears and in my eyes,
a four of fish and finger pies
in summer meanwhile back
Behind the shelter in the middle of the round-a-bout
The pretty nurse is selling poppies from a tray.
And though she feels as if she's in a play
she is anyway.

In Penny Lane, the barber shaves another customer,
we see the Banker sitting waiting for a trim
and the fireman rushes in
from the pouring rain—
very strange.

Penny Lane is in my ears and in my eyes,
there beneath the blue suburban skies
I sit, and meanwhile back

Penny Lane is in my ears and in my eyes,
there beneath the blue suburban skies . . .
Penny Lane!

CHAPTER FOUR

THE UNIVERSE

PAINT IT BLACK

Mick Jagger and Keith Richard

I see a red door and I want it painted black,
No colors anymore, I want them to turn black.
I see the girls walk by dressed in their summer clothes,
I have to turn my head until my darkness goes.

I see a line of cars and they're all painted black,
With flowers and my love both never to come back.
I see people turn their heads and quickly look away,
Like a new-born baby, it just happens everyday.

I look inside myself, and see my heart turn black,
I see my red door and must have it painted black.
Maybe then I'll fade away and not have to face the facts,
Not easy to face it up when your whole world is black.

No more will my green sea go turn a deeper blue,
I could not foresee this thing happening to you.
If I look hard enough into the setting sun,
My love will laugh with me before the morning comes.

I see a red door and I want it painted black,
No colors anymore, I want them to turn black.
I see the girls come by dressed in their summer clothes.
I have to turn my head until my darkness goes.

I want you painted, painted black,
Black as night, black as coal.
I want to see the sun
Blotted out from the sky.
I want to see you painted
            painted
                painted
                    painted
                      black.

1. What is the intensely personal and traumatic loss the speaker has recently suffered? Does he move from that experience to a *world* view that is black? Discuss the term "nihilism" as it applies to the poem. Weigh any evidence in the poem that the speaker now finds blackness on the personal, social and metaphysical levels of existence.

2. Are there any signs in the poem of hope for the speaker's condition?

3. Is there a thematic development in the poem? If so, is it linear or cyclical? Does the poem have a climax?

4. Discuss the symbolic values of colors and of objects, such as the door and the sun. Discuss the symbolic values of actions, such as painting, facing and turning away.

5. Read a poem by Wallace Stevens called "Domination of Black." What relationships do you see?

BLACKBIRD

John Lennon and Paul McCartney

Blackbird singing in the dead of night
Take these broken wings and learn to fly.
All your life
You were only waiting for this moment to arise.

Blackbird singing in the dead of night
Take these sunken eyes and learn to see.
All your life
You were only waiting for this moment to be free.

Blackbird fly, blackbird fly
Into the light of the dark black night.
Blackbird fly, blackbird fly
Into the light of the dark black night.

Blackbird singing in the dead of night
Take these broken wings and learn to fly.
All your life
You were only waiting for this moment to arise
You were only waiting for this moment to arise
You were only waiting for this moment to arise.

1. In literature, blackbirds are traditional harbingers of death. Can you remember any poems or other literary pieces that used the blackbird in such a fashion? How many aspects of this poem's first line link the poem with death? How many aspects of the rest of the poem?

2. a. What does a blackbird's "song" sound like? Does this visual-audial image of the blackbird singing fit with the other imagery in the poem?
   b. How many contrasts can you find in the poem?

3. Is there any allusion to the famous Egyptian mythological bird called the Phoenix? What meanings would such an allusion lend to the poem?

4. Why does the speaker offer wings that are broken and eyes that are sunken?

5. Read Wallace Stevens' "Thirteen Ways of Looking at a Blackbird." Which one of Stevens' thirteen views of the bird best protrays Lennon-McCartney's blackbird?

A WHITER SHADE OF PALE

Keith Reid and Gary Brooker

We skipped the light fandango
And turned cartwheels cross the floor.
I was feeling kind of seasick
But the crowd called out for more.
The room was humming harder
As the ceiling flew away
When we called out for another drink
The waiter brought a tray
And so it was that later
As the miller told his tale
That her face at first just ghostly
Turned a whiter shade of pale

She said "There is no reason
And the truth is plain to see,"
But I wandered through my playing cards
And would not let her be
One of sixteen vestal virgins
Who were leaving for the coast
And although my eyes were open
They might just have well been closed.
And so it was that later
As the miller told his tale
That her face at first just ghostly
Turned a whiter shade of pale.

1. Identify the first word "we."

2. What kind of a dance is the fandango?

3. What cliché does the opening line parody?

4. Do the cartwheels fit in with the fandango? To what extent is the speaker being literal?

5. Why does the speaker say he felt *sea*sick? Why not just sick?

6. Do you get the feeling that the room, and not the speaker, was dancing?

7. Was the crowd a particular group (as the "in-crowd") or an anonymous crowd?

8. What did the crowd call out for more of?

9. Was the room actually humming, as with life and activity, or was the humming something in the speaker's ears?

10. Which ceiling flew away—the room's or the speaker's?

11. In line 9, what is the significance of "later"?

12. Who was the miller and what was his tale? Is the line a reference to Chaucer's *Canterbury Tales?*

13. Why would "her" face turn pale? If she had heard Chaucer's miller's tale, would her face have turned white or red?

14. In stanza two, what does the girl's statement refer to?

15. Who was she talking to?

16. How does one wander through playing cards? Could this be a metaphor?

17. Does the "But" from "But I wandered. . ." indicate the relationship of playing cards to truth? To the girl's statement?

18. What wouldn't the speaker let the girl be—
    a virgin?
    a vestal virgin?
    one of the sixteen vestal virgins?
    leaving for the coast?

19. What is a vestal virgin, and what place does the term have in the poem? Is it related to the playing cards? To the dance? To a suggested sexual encounter?

20. Why might the speaker's eyes have been closed? Is this a metaphorical reference to other such metaphors as his being blind, or asleep, or dead?

21. Why are the last four lines so significant as to be repeated as a chorus?

22. Can the miller have identity beyond Chaucer's miller?

23. Why specifically a whiter shade of pale? Why not just pale, or just white? What does the emphasized whiteness suggest?

24. Could "shade" be linked with "ghostly" and "tale"? How much of the poem's imagery is ghostlike? How much is hallucinative or dreamlike? Does the term "surrealism" apply here?

25. Can the words "there is no reason" apply also to the poem as a whole? Then what about "the truth is plain to see"?

26. What does the poem mean? Some poetry defies logic. In some poems there is no literal statement. The meaning consists of the reader-listener's collective impressions of the poem's collective images. Can you put the poem's images together in some kind of a meaningful pattern?

27. Do you think the principal unifying agent of "A Whiter Shade of Pale" might be the song's music?

28. If a person had been on a drunken, whirling spree, and he tried to recount it for you the next morning, would you get a rational and coherent story, or would you get a series of fragments, united only by his voice in telling you and by the particular kind of consciousness he had on the previous night?

29. What is the particular kind of consciousness of the drunken person? Is it related to other forms of consciousness?

30. Drunkenness is looked on by some as a celebration of life, by others as a form of death. The dance too, from the earliest ritual, has been connected both with life celebrations and with death ceremonies. Which do you think fits better into the context of this poem?

WHITE RABBIT

Grace Slick

One pill makes you larger
And one pill makes you small.
And the ones that mother gives you
Don't do anything at all.
Go ask Alice
When she's ten feet tall.

And if you go chasing rabbits
And you know you're going to fall.
Tell 'em a hookah smoking caterpillar
Has given you the call
Call Alice
When she was just small.

When men on the chessboard
Get up and tell you where to go.
And you've just had some kind of mushroom
And your mind is moving low.
Go ask Alice
I think she'll know.

When logic and proportion
Have fallen sloppy dead,
And the White Knight is talking backwards
And the Red Queen's lost her head

Remember what the dormouse said:
"Heed your head.
Heed your head.
Heed your head."

1. Look up the allusions to Lewis Carroll's two books—*Alice in Wonderland* (1865), and *Through the Looking Glass* (1871). Do all the allusions relate to specific events in Carroll's tales or are some treated differently? How much does the poem's meaning depend on the reader-listener's knowledge of Carroll's stories?

2. We (of modern society) have not fallen down a rabbit's hole, but does the poem become a metaphor of a modern experience? Besides the obvious references to drugs, does the poem communicate on other metaphorical levels? For example, are there any parallels between the situation of the person addressed in the poem as "you" and the situation of modern, existential man? Does the twentieth-century concept of "the absurd" apply here?

3. Compare this poem with "A Whiter Shade of Pale." Concentrate especially on the application of the term "surrealism" to each.

THE BUTCHER

Leonard Cohen

I came upon a butcher
He was slaughtering a lamb
I accused him there
With his tortured lamb
He said "Listen to me, child
I am what I am
And you, you are my only son."

Well, I found a silver needle
I put it into my arm
It did some good
Did some harm.
But the nights were cold
And it almost kept me warm
How come the night is long?

I saw some flowers growing up
Where that lamb fell down
Was I supposed to praise my lord
Make some kind of joyful sound?
He said, "Listen, listen to me now
I go round and round,
And you, you are my only child."

Do not leave me now,
Do not leave me now,
I'm broken down
From a recent fall.
Blood upon my body
And ice upon my soul
Lead on, my son, it is your world.

1. Compare this poem with "Story of Isaac." Can you find any parallels? Which theme has a broader application?

2. Who is the speaker in the poem? Who is he accusing? What is the accusation? What is the reply?

3. Can you find biblical allusions in the poem? Could the poem be about the relationship between man and God? Between God and Messiah? Can you relate the poem to the "God is dead" school of theology?

4. The Christian tradition is predicated on a linear theory of history. That is, before Christ, history was a cycle endlessly repeating itself. After Christ, however, history became linear, in that it was now directed to a specific end (the day of judgment and resurrection). Can you find evidence of cyclical and linear patterns of history in the poem?

5. At the end of John Milton's *Paradise Regained*, God says to Messiah, "Now enter, and begin to save mankind." Compare this line with the final line of "The Butcher." Does Cohen's line mean the same thing? Can you detect any differences?

THE STRANGER SONG

Leonard Cohen

It's true that all the men you knew were dealers
who said they were through with dealing
Every time you gave them shelter
I know that kind of man
It's hard to hold the hand of anyone
who is reaching for the sky just to surrender.

And then sweeping up the jokers that he left behind
you find he did not leave you very much
not even laughter
Like any dealer he was watching for the card
that is so high and wild
he'll never need to deal another
He was just some Joseph looking for a manger
He was just some Joseph looking for a manger.

And then leaning on your window sill
he'll say one day you caused his will
to weaken with your love and warmth and shelter
And then taking from his wallet
an old schedule of trains, he'll say
I told you when I came I was a stranger
I told you when I came I was a stranger.

But now another stranger seems
to want you to ignore his dreams
as though they were the burden of some other
O you've seen that man before
his golden arm dispatching cards
but now it's rusted from the elbow to the finger
And he wants to trade the game he plays for shelter
Yes he wants to trade the game he knows for shelter.

You hate to watch another tired man
lay down his hand
like he was giving up the holy game of poker
And while he talks his dreams to sleep
you notice there's a highway
that is curling up like smoke above his shoulder
It's curling just like smoke above his shoulder.

You tell him to come in sit down
but something makes you turn around
The door is open you can't close your shelter
You try the handle of the road
It opens do not be afraid
It's you my love, you who are the stranger
It is you my love, you who are the stranger.

Well, I've been waiting, I was sure
we'd meet between the trains we're waiting for
I think it's time to board another
Please understand, I never had a secret chart
to get me to the heart of this
or any other matter
Well he talks like this
you don't know what he's after
When he speaks like this,
you don't know what he's after.

Let's meet tomorrow if you choose
upon the shore, beneath the bridge
that they are building on some endless river
Then he leaves the platform
for the sleeping car that's warm
You realize, he's only advertising one more shelter
And it comes to you, he never was a stranger
And you say ok the bridge or someplace later.

And then sweeping up the jokers
that he left behind
you find he did not leave you very much
not even laughter
Like any dealer he was watching for the card
that is so high and wild he'll never need
to deal another
He was just some Joseph looking for a manger
He was just some Joseph looking for a manger.

And leaning on your window sill
he'll say one day you caused his will
to weaken with your love and warmth and shelter
And then taking from his wallet
an old schedule of trains
he'll say, I told you when I came I was a stranger
I told you when I came I was a stranger.

1. Is love like a game of cards? What about the theory of love expounded by Dr. Erich Fromm in *The Art of Loving* (1956)? Is love merely another game people play?

2. Discuss religious imagery. Is the highway a halo? At what points do the religious and card-playing images meet? Why do they meet?

3. What effect does the repetition of two entire stanzas have on the meaning of the poem?

4. The river, the highway, the railroad tracks: Do they contrast to love, warmth, and shelter?

5. The stranger is an archetypal figure. How many strangers can you remember from your encounters with literature, mythology, or folklore, with films, comic books, or television programs? What characteristics do the strangers have in common? Are there parallels in the way each functions in his respective environment?

   Discuss the figure of the stranger in this poem. Is his function like that of the archetypal stranger? Can you find any differences? Is there more than one stranger?

CRUCIFIXION

Phil Ochs

And the night comes again to the circle-studded sky
The stars settle slowly, in loneliness they lie
Till the universe explodes as a falling star is raised
The planets are paralyzed, the mountains are amazed
But they all glow brighter from the brilliance of the blaze
With the speed of insanity, then, he dies.

In the green fields of turning a baby is born
His cries crease the wind and mingle with the morn
An assault upon the order, the changing of the guard
Chosen for a challenge that's hopelessly hard
And the only single sign is the sighing of the stars
But to the silence of distance they're sworn.

So dance, dance, dance
Teach us to be true
Come dance, dance, dance
'Cause we love you.

Images of innocence charge him to go on
But the decadence of history is looking for a pawn
To a nightmare of knowledge he opens up the gate
A blinding revelation is served upon his plate
That beneath the greatest love is a hurricane of hate
And God help the critic of the dawn.

So he stands on the sea and he shouts to the shore
But the louder that he screams the longer he's ignored
For the wine of oblivion is drunk to the dregs
And the merchants of the masses almost have to be begged
Till the giant is aware that someone's pulling at his leg
And someone is tapping at the door.

So dance, dance, dance
Teach us to be true
Come dance, dance, dance
'Cause we love you.

Then his message gathers meaning and it spreads across
        the land
The rewarding of the fame is the following of the man
But ignorance is everywhere and people have their way
And success is an enemy to the losers of the day
In the shadows of the churches who knows what they pray
And blood is the language of the band.

The Spanish bulls are beaten, the crowd is soon beguiled
The matador is beautiful, a symphony of style
Excitement is ecstatic, passion places bets
Gracefully he bows to ovations that he gets
But the hands that are applauding are slippery with sweat
And saliva is falling from their smiles.

So dance, dance, dance
Teach us to be true
Come dance, dance, dance
'Cause we love you.

Then this overflow of life is crushed into a liar
The gentle soul is ripped apart and tossed into the fire
It's the burial of beauty, it's the victory of night
Truth becomes a tragedy limping from the light
The heavens are horrified, they stagger from the sight
And the cross is trembling with desire.

They say they can't believe it, it's a sacrilegious shame
Now who would want to hurt such a hero of the game
But you know I predicted it, I knew he had to fall
How did it happen, I hope his suffering was small

Tell me every detail, I've got to know it all
And do you have a picture of the pain?

So dance, dance, dance
Teach us to be true
Come dance, dance, dance
'Cause we love you.

Time takes her toll and the memory fades
But his glory is growing in the magic that he made
Reality is ruined, there is nothing more to fear
The drama is distorted to what they want to hear
Swimming in their sorrow in the twisting of a tear
As they wait for the new thrill parade.

The eyes of the rebel have been branded by the blind
To the safety of sterility the threat has been refined
The child was created to the slaughter house he's led
So good to be alive when the eulogies are read
The climax of emotion, the worship of the dead
As the cycle of sacrifice unwinds.

So dance, dance, dance
Teach us to be true
Come dance, dance, dance
'Cause we love you.

And the night comes again to the circle-studded sky
The stars settle slowly, in loneliness they lie
Till the universe explodes as a falling star is raised
The planets are paralyzed, the mountains are amazed
But they all glow brighter from the brilliance of the blaze
With the speed of insanity, then, he dies.

1. Is the poem a narrative of Christ's life or a history of Christianity? Could it be both? Could it be both and still more?

2. In many works of literature, a character is depicted in some way as to bear resemblance to Christ. Hence, many different kinds of characters are called Christ-figures. Show how the process is reversed in this poem.

3. Compare the reactions of the universe with the reactions of society to the birth, life, and death of the poem's hero.

4. Why do you think the first stanza is repeated at the end of the poem?

5. Does the poem suggest any particular theory of history?

6. Note the use of irony in the chorus. How does it characterize society? Is irony used in other places in the poem?

7. In the eighth stanza (not counting the chorus) identify the "I" of "I predicted it."

8. Discuss evidence of sadism and voyeurism in the poem.

9. Look again at the poem's title. Exactly what does it refer to?

10. Can you find any links between this song and the album *Jesus Christ Superstar?*

SUZANNE

Leonard Cohen

Suzanne takes you down to her place near the river
You can hear the boats go by
You can spend the night beside her
And you know that she's half crazy
But that's why you want to be there
And she feeds you tea and oranges
That come all the way from China
And just when you mean to tell her
That you have no love to give her
Then she gets you on her wavelength
And she lets the river answer
That you've always been her lover
And you want to travel with her
And you want to travel blind
And you know that she will trust you
For you've touched her perfect body with your mind.

And Jesus was a sailor
When he walked upon the water
And he spent a long time watching
From his lonely wooden tower
And when he knew for certain
Only drowning men could see him
He said "All men will be sailors then
Until the sea shall free them"
But he himself was broken
Long before the sky would open
Forsaken, almost human
He sank beneath your wisdom like a stone

And you want to travel with him
And you want to travel blind
And you think maybe you'll trust him
For he's touched your perfect body with his mind.

Now Suzanne takes your hand
And she leads you to the river
She is wearing rags and feathers
From Salvation Army counters
And the sun pours down like honey
On our lady of the harbour
And she shows you where to look
Among the garbage and the flowers
There are heroes in the seaweed
There are children in the morning
They are leaning out for love
And they will lean that way forever
While Suzanne holds the mirror

And you want to travel with her
And you want to travel blind
And you know you can trust her
For she's touched your perfect body with her mind.

1. The poem talks about two people: Suzanne and Jesus. Both of them are associated with water; Suzanne lives by the harbor, Jesus was a sailor. The poem says each can be trusted because he has touched your body with his mind. Do these relationships suggest anything about salvation? If so, what kind of salvation is being proposed?

2. Suzanne is described as a half-crazy woman who wears rags and feathers from Salvation Army counters. Many primitive cultures regard a madman as someone holy who has been touched by the gods. Is this the kind of madness Suzanne has?

3. "For you've touched her perfect body with your mind." "For she's touched your perfect body with her mind." Christian theology traditionally differentiates between eros (human or physical love) and agape (divine or spiritual love). Is the love Suzanne has to offer sacred or profane? Could it be both?

4. The sea is a traditional symbol of life, death, and rebirth. The second stanza speaks of men as sailors, of men drowning, of the sea as the means by which men will be freed. Are these metaphors?

CALIFORNIA DREAMIN'

John Phillips

All the leaves are brown,
And the sky is grey.
I've been for a walk
On a winter's day.
I'd be safe and warm
If I was in L. A.
California dreamin'
On such a winter's day.

Stopped into a church
I passed along the way.
Oh, I got down on my knees
And I pretended to pray.
You know, the preacher likes the cold.
He knows I'm gonna stay.
California dreamin'
On such a winter's day.

All the leaves are brown,
And the sky is grey.
I've been for a walk
On a winter's day.
If I didn't tell her,
I could leave today.
California dreamin'
On such a winter's day.
On such a winter's day.

1. Is the poem's simplicity deceptive? Is there anything beyond the literal level?

2. Why is the season winter? Why does the poet emphasize the season?

3. Why did the speaker stop in church? Why did he pretend to pray?

4. Discuss the contrast set up in the poem between secular paradise and religious paradise. How many images are contrasted to L. A.? Can we interpret the choice of paradise as a comment on our times?

5. Compare this poem with "October Song." Concentrate on image and statement.

BIRD ON THE WIRE

Leonard Cohen

Like a bird on the wire
Like a drunk in a midnight choir
I have tried in my way to be free
Like a worm on a hook
Like a knight from some old-fashioned book
I have saved all my ribbons for thee
> If I have been unkind
> I hope that you can just let it go by
> If I have been untrue,
> I hope you know it was never to you.

Like a baby stillborn
Like a beast with his horn
I have torn everyone who reached out for me
But I swear by this song
And by all that I have done wrong
I will make it all up to thee.
> I saw a beggar leaning on his wooden crutch
> He said to me, "You must not ask for so much."
> And a pretty woman leaning in her darkened door,
> She cried to me, "Hey, why not ask for more?"

Like a bird on the wire
Like a drunk in a midnight choir
I have tried in my way to be free.

1. The speaker refers to himself in three sets of similes. Discuss the kinds of comparisons he makes.

2. What is the relationship between the two images within each set of similes? Here is a riddle:

QUESTION: How is a stillborn baby like a beast with his horn?
ANSWER   : Each tears everyone who reaches out for it.

Metaphor is the process of seeing a likeness between two dissimilar things. Of course, some things are more dissimilar than others. What is your opinion of the relative dissimilarity between the components of Cohen's metaphors?

3. What comment upon the nature of freedom do the first three lines of the poem make?

4. The speaker seems to be caught between crippled beggars and pretty women. Is his situation a universal one? Notice that both the beggar and the woman are leaning on something. What does the speaker lean on? What comment on the nature of freedom do these lines of the poem make?

5.   Hup, two, three, four,
         Hup, two,
         Three,
         Four,
         Halt!
         Left turn!
         Right turn!
         About face!
         About face!
         About face!
         About face!
         Abou
         Tf
         Ace
         !

Judging from the Cohen poems you've encountered in this book, can you see the above as a metaphor of Cohen's polemic method?

OCTOBER SONG

Robin Williamson

I'll sing you this October song
Oh, there is no song before it
The words and tune are none of my own
But my joys and sorrows bore it

Beside the sea the brambly briars
In the still of evening
Birds fly out behind the sun
And with them I'll be leaving

The fallen leaves that jewel the ground
They know the art of dying
And leave with joy their glad gold hearts
In the scarlet shadows lying

When hunger calls my footsteps home
The morning follows after
I swim the seas within my mind
And the pine-trees laugh green laughter

I met a man whose name was Time
And he said, "I must be going"
But just how long ago that was
I have no way of knowing.

Sometimes I want to murder time
Sometimes when my heart's aching
But mostly I just stroll along
The path that he is taking

1. Why an "October" song? What is the symbolic function of the season?

2. The speaker tells us that the leaves "know the art of dying." Does this suggest the universal pattern of nature? What evidence do we have that the speaker is like the leaves?

3. Where is the peace that the speaker has found?

4. How do the external physical images mirror the speaker's mind?

5. What is the relationship between the speaker's state of mind and the condition of the figures he mentions in the third stanza?

6. What is the difference between the speaker's sorrows and the sorrow of the speaker in "Paint It Black"?

wear your love like heaven

Donovan Leitch

colour in sky prussian blue
scarlet fleece changes hue
crimson ball sinks from view

wear your love like heaven
wear your love like heaven
wear your love like heaven

lord kiss me once more
fill me with song
allah kiss me once more
that i may that i may
wear my love like heaven
wear my love like heaven

colour sky havana lake
colour sky rose carmethene
alizarian crimson

wear your love like heaven
wear your love like heaven
wear your love like heaven

lord kiss me once more
fill me with song
allah kiss me once more
that i may that i may
wear my love like heaven
wear my love like heaven

can i believe what i see
all i have wished for will be
all our race proud and free

wear your love like heaven
wear your love like heaven
wear your love like heaven

lord kiss me once more
fill me with song
allah kiss me once more
that i may that i may
wear my love like heaven
wear my love like heaven

carmine

1. "wear your love like heaven"
   Wear your love as heaven wears love.
   Wear your love as you would wear heaven.
   Wear your love as if love were heaven.
   Wear your love as if heaven were love.
   Wear your love as. . .

   Discuss all the implications of the line.

2. The speaker addresses the lord and allah. Is he calling on many gods or is he implying that all gods are one?

3. Scarlet, crimson, rose, carmine . . . what color *is* red? The colors in this poem are all given precise specific names. A dictionary tells something of their differences; a paint shop would reveal even more. In the context of the poem, do you think these names are simply different ways of saying "red" or "blue," or is the naming significant?

4. Notice how much the poem employs repetition (of words, lines, stanzas). Repetition of important words, phrases, and concepts is an integral part of the ritual of worship. Does the poem seem similar to a litany or a prayer? Could the poem itself be an act of worship? If this interpretation is valid, can you determine what the religious viewpoint of the poem is? Can you deduce anything of the nature of its deity?

5.   can i believe what i see
         all i have wished for will be
         all our race proud and free

   This stanza appears in a climactic position in the poem and, in addition, is the only stanza that is not repeated in any way. Does the rest of the poem point to this stanza? Do the lines suggest the result of wearing your love like heaven?

THE TINKER AND THE CRAB

Donovan Leitch

On the windy beach the sun is shining through with weather fair
White horses riding on the seas pasture onto the sand
Over the Dunes came a travelling man
Sack on back Wild flowers in his hand
Old rusty cans, pebbles 'bedded in the sand stand and stare

Scratching his beard through the grass he steered his sandy shoe
Disappearing in the dips pondering and wandering along
Nice as you please comes the travelling man
Drinking a bottle of milk in his hand
Speaking to no one in particular but happily

Down where the gulls dance driftwood lying drying for the fire
Yellow beak and sleek now the gulls are crying flying higher
Out from the sea came a little green Crab
Taking the Sun the morning being very drab
Old rusty cans, pebbles 'bedded in the sand stand and stare

The Tinker and the Crab
The Tinker and the Crab
The Tinker and the Crab

1. Nineteenth century Romantic poets were much concerned with the concept of man in relation to nature. Nature was the great teacher, both of wisdom and ethics, while the city, preoccupied with industrial mechanism, corrupted and debased men. Only by being in close harmony with nature could men achieve the holiness of which the Romantics were convinced that all men were capable. Can you find evidence of this kind of Romanticism in "The Tinker and the Crab"? Through which images are the worlds of man and nature linked?

2. Note the rhythm of the final three lines. List all the words with "s" sounds. Are these auditory images? How does sound function as a link between form and content?

3. Why is the only human being in the poem a Tinker? Consider the nature of a Tinker's occupation and way of life. Does this suggest why the poet chose a Tinker?

4. Notice the verb tenses. What idea about time is the poet trying to express?

STARFISH-ON-THE-TOAST

Donovan Leitch

Fine rock-pooling Coast
This Starfish-On-The-Toast
The men in the Crabbin' boats they cry

Far across the Harbour
And round the Sandy Cove,
The Shepherd wi' his pipe and Sheepy-Drove

Big Cloud Tumbling high
The Amazing Flying Sky
How the gulls are pillaging the town

Fanfaring Daffodilly trumpetingly small
All along the Bathing hut wall

Far along the empty beach the Tide has left a World
Old men in tweed find study there

Holding Whelks and Periwinkles tingling in his hand
Little does he know they hold him too

1. What other things in the poem have consciousness besides the people? What does this say about the poet's world view?

2. How many worlds is the poet talking about? What constitutes a world?

3. How does the poet make visual perspective work in the poem? Can you find similarities to the techniques of the telescope and the microscope? Consider how each device enlarges our vision. What kinds of visual perspectives do these man-made instruments give? Does the last line give a still different kind of "vision"?

4. Compare Donovan's poem with the following poem by Alfred, Lord Tennyson:

FLOWER IN THE CRANNIED WALL

Flower in the crannied wall,
I pluck you out of the crannies,
I hold you here, root and all, in my hand,
Little flower—but *if* I could understand
What you are, root and all, and all in all,
I should know what God and man is.

THE LULLABY OF SPRING

Donovan Leitch

rain has showered far her drip
splash and trickle running
plant has flowered in the sand
shell and pebble sunning

so begins another spring
green leaves and of berries
chiff-chaff eggs are painted by
motherbird eating cherries

in a misty tangled sky
fast a wind is blowing
in a newborn rabbit's heart
river life is flowing

so begins another spring
green leaves and of berries
chiff-chaff eggs are painted by
motherbird eating cherries

from the dark and whetted soil
petals are unfolding
from the stony village kirk
easter bells of old ring

so begins another spring
green leaves and of berries
chiff-chaff eggs are painted by
motherbird eating cherries

1. Which images are primarily visual? Which are auditory? Which are tactile? Which convey the sense of movement? What is the percentage of concreteness to abstraction in the poem? Is the poem any more than a collection of concrete images of spring? *Should* a poem be any more than a collection of images?

2. Take a close look at the structure: six stanzas. Three sets of parallels, interrupted and closed by the refrain. All *living* signs of spring. What kinds of parallels does the poet establish? How does he use syntax to point out the parallelism? Does the fifth stanza suggest a further parallel event?

3. Why do you think the poet used such unusual words as "kirk" and "chiff-chaff"? What do they add to the poem?

4. Why a "misty tangled sky"? Can you picture it?

5. Compare this poem with the Medieval lyric, "Sumer is icumen in," which follows.

SUMER IS ICUMEN IN

Sumer is icumen in;
    Lhude sing, cuccu!
Groweth sed, and bloweth med,
    And springth the wude nu.
        Sing, cuccu!
Awe bleteth after lomb,
    Lhouth after calve cu;
Bulluc sterteth, bucke verteth;
    Murie sing, cuccu!
        Cuccu! cuccu!
    Wel singes thu, cuccu;
    Ne swik thu naver nu.

ISLE OF ISLAY

Donovan Leitch

How high the gulls fly o'er Islay
How sad the farm lad deep in play
Felt like a grain on your sand

How well the sheeps bell music makes
Rovin' the cliff when fancy takes
Felt like a tide left me here

How blest the forest with birds song
How neat the cut peat laid so long
Felt like a seed on your land

1. Why are almost all of the words monosyllabic? Compare this characteristic with its use in Mick Jagger's "As Tears Go By."

2. In Aristotelian logic, a "syllogism" is, as Aristotle himself defined it, "a discourse in which, certain things being posited, something else follows them by necessity."

    Basic syllogisms have three steps, and might read something like this:

    all A is B

    C is A

    $\therefore$ C is B

    Deductive logic moves from the general to the specific, as opposed to the inductive process, which moves from specific to general.

    a. Each of Donovan's stanzas in "Isle of Islay" has three lines. Can you consider them "steps"? Is there any movement? If so, is the movement deductive or inductive? Is it "logical"?

    b. Between any premises or set of data and a conclusion there is a gap that must be jumped, even if the conclusion seems to "follow by necessity." Does the third line in each stanza in any way indicate a conclusion? If so, do you think it follows "by necessity"?

3. What are your own thoughts on mysticism? Discuss them with other people. Are there any religious, cultural, or social factors that seem to be consistent influences on a person's concept of mysticism?

    Now, perhaps these concepts can be used as a way of approaching this poem. Would you say that it is an attempt to express a mystical experience? What gap must the mystic jump?

4. Note certain ambiguities: to whom does "your" refer? The speaker's loved one? The reader? God? All three? How would the mystic answer the question? "Felt." What exactly is felt? Through what sense? Is ambiguity a necessary consequence of someone trying to convey a mystical message? Can you reconcile the ambiguities with the stark simplicity of the poem's structure?

5. Three stanzas, three lines. Consider the symbolic (and mystical) properties of the number three.

6.

Reread question number 9 of the questions following "The Continuing Story of Bungalow Bill." Does the configuration of "Isle of Islay" affect the meaning of the poem?

DONOVAN'S POEMS: AN OVERVIEW

These five poems by Donovan are all from a two-record album called *a gift from a flower to a garden.* In a headnote to the volume, Donovan dedicates his poems to those of his age group, an age group which is entering marriage, and to their children. Considering these poems as part of a group of related poems directed to a specific audience, go back through them, examining them for similarities in technique, imagery, symbolism, and theme.

a. Discuss the poems in terms of rhyme: end rhyme, slant rhyme, internal rhyme, feminine rhyme, and so on. Notice the use of alliteration, assonance, and onomatopoeia. Consider metrical rhythms and repetition. Do sounds and rhythms constitute auditory images? Are these devices more than ornamental in these poems?

b. Discuss imagery in the poems. Can you find similarities in the kinds of images used? In the way images are used? Which images achieve the force of symbols? Can you relate imagery to theme?

c. Discuss mysticism in the poems. Can you find evidence of mysticism in all of them? Could "Isle of Islay" in any way be considered a culminating expression of mysticism? Do you think there is a connection between mysticism and Romanticism?

d. Can you formulate a literal statement for each poem? Is it possible to formulate a thematic statement for all of them as a group? Could the speaker of the poems be considered a teacher? Could he be considered a prophet? If you think this is true, what is his teaching, and his prophecy?

HAMPSTEAD INCIDENT

Donovan Leitch

Standing by the Everyman
Digging the rigging on my sails
Rain fell through sounds of harpsichords
Through the spell of fairy tales

The heath was hung in magic mists
And gentle dripping glades
I'll taste the tastes until my mind
Drifts from this scene and fades

In the nighttime

Crystals sparkle in the grass
I polish them with thought
On my lash there in my eye
A star of light is caught

Fortunes told in grains of sand
Here I am is all I know
Can be stuck in children's hair
Everywhere I go

In the nighttime
In the nighttime

Gypsy is the clown of love
I paint his face a smile
Anyone we ever make
We always make in style

Strange young girls with radar screens
And hands as quick as pain
I want just now later on maybe
And even then I'll wait

In the nighttime
In the nighttime

Standing by the Everyman
Digging the rigging on my sails
Rain fell through sounds of harpsichords
Through the spell of fairy tales

The heath was hung in magic mists
And gentle dripping glades
I'll taste the tastes until my mind
Drifts from this scene and fades

In the nighttime
In the nighttime

KOEEOADDI THERE

Robin Williamson

the natural cards revolve
    ever changing
seeded elsewhere planted
    in the garden fair grow
    trees, grow trees

tongues of the sheer wind
    setting your foot where
    the sand is untrodden
    the ocean that only
    begins

listen a woman with a
    bulldozer built this
    house of now
carving away the mountain
    whose name is your
    childhood home
we were trying to buy it
    buy it buy it
someone was found killed
    there all bones bones
    dry bones
earth water fire and air
    met together in a
    garden fair
put in a basket bound
    with skin if you
    answer this riddle
    you'll never begin

born in a house where the
    doors shut tight
shadowy fingers on the
    curtains at night
cherry tree blossom head
    high snow

a busy man's road where I
    wasn't to go
I used to sit on the garden
    wall
say hello to people going
    by so tall
hello to the postman's
    stubbly skin
hello to the baker's stubbly
    grin
mrs thompson gave me a
    bear
brigitte and some people
    lived upstairs
skating on happy valley
    pond
various ministers and guards
    stood around
the ice was nice hello the
    invisible brethren
and there was a tent you
    played cards with the
soldiers in, "don't worry we
    won't send anyone
after you" they screamed

but me and licorice saw the
    last of them one
misty twisty day

across the mournful
    morning moor motoring
    away
singing ladybird ladybird
    what is your wish
your wish is not granted
    unless it's a fish
your wish is not granted
    unless it's a dish
a fish on a dish is that
    what you wish

earth water fire and air
    met together in a
    garden fair
put in a basket bound
    with skin if you
    answer this riddle
    you'll never begin

CHAPTER FIVE

Discussions on Poetic Meaning

STATEMENT

A poem stands between the poet and his audience, but it is meant to join, not to separate. A poem is the middle ground or medium through which the poet conveys something of himself to his audience. Words are the stuff that makes poems, and poets can use words in a number of ways in order to communicate their feelings and ideas. One way—the most obvious way but only sometimes the nearest—is to communicate them directly and overtly. To this way we'll give the name "statement."

> He who rides with the klan
> Is a devil and not a man.

. . . .

> I love you.

. . . .

> Speed kills!

. . . .

> It was a beautiful garden.

. . . .

These are statements—overt and direct. Whole poems can be fashioned in this way, and have been throughout the poetic tradition. William Wordsworth provides us with a famous example.

> My heart leaps up when I behold
>   a rainbow in the sky:
> So was it when my life began;
> So is it now I am a man;
> So be it when I shall grow old,
>   Or let me die!

> The child is father of the man,
> And I could wish my days to be
> Bound each to each by natural piety.

Many songs we hear today on the radio and on records are fairly overt and direct statements. Often these are sentimental and trite, but not always. A poem can take advantage of its straightforwardness, its nakedness, and its simplicity in order to achieve real power. Stephen Stills' song "For What It's Worth" is one such powerful statement. Similarly, but in another sphere, Tim Hardin's words in "If I Were a Carpenter" achieve the gentle, simple power of the love lyric.

Direct, overt, simple. Since these terms are relative and their application is subjective, review the songs in this book (and compare with any other songs or poems you are familiar with), determining for yourself which ones correspond to the kind of poem that is described above.

.   .   .   .   .

What have you been able to discover? Have you found that few are "pure" statements? Have you found that some don't seem to make any statement at all, or at least they don't make a statement that you can paraphrase? Have you found that some are simple statements that also seem to suggest more than what they say? Have you thought about "levels"? Most poems have a literal meaning, based on the ordinary, denotative signification of the words and the relationships between them. But for many poems the literal meaning is only one level of meaning, the surface level. We can also use the term "statement" to refer to this level of the poem. The following sections will discuss layers of meaning beneath the surface.

IMAGE

Language is a social medium; it is meant to bring people together. But each person is unique, with his own attitudes and concepts, and with unique experiences. Moreover, a person brings to bear on each language encounter his individual attitudes, concepts, and experiences. Perfect communication is an ideal we perhaps can never reach but, hopefully, we will continue to try.

If I have seen a beautiful garden yesterday, and I want to communicate my experience to you, I have a few options. I could bring you to the garden and let you experience it directly, but this is not always possible. I can say to you, "It was a beautiful garden." I am *telling* you. But how do you respond to my communication? You will have to take my word that the garden was beautiful. You may think of gardens that you have been to and have judged as being beautiful. You may be a professional gardener, have your own ideas about what makes a beautiful garden, and the mere mention of the word will elicit a profusion of responses. Or perhaps you've never seen one before. We may be thinking of quite different things at the close of my statement, if, indeed, you are thinking of gardens at all.

In order to more fully convey the beauty of the garden, I can describe it. Here I will use images, words that you will be able to receive through your senses. Consequently, I will describe the smell of honeysuckle, the spectrum of colors, the drone of bees, the smooth feel of closely mown grass, the fresh, gurgling sound of the running stream, the symmetry of flower arrangements, and so on. Through these physical details, these images, you are able to respond more fully to what I have experienced. You are able to experience the garden vicariously, and are thereby better able to conclude for yourself that it was indeed beautiful. I have *shown* you, and we have more fully interacted.

An image is a bridge between the poet and his audience. It is made of concrete. Our experience of it is sensory, and this is another dimension of communication.

A poem is a special kind of language encounter in which images are a vital ingredient. Their function is much more than decorative. Poets use images to communicate ideas, to express emotions, to create an experience the reader can share. A poetic image is the reproduction in words of an object that can be experienced by one or more of the senses, or a reproduction of the sensory experience itself. When the poet shows you a gurgling brook, you can picture the brook—a visual image of an object. The gurgling sound you hear through the image is a sensory experience itself. Most images are visual, but the poet may also communicate other sensory experiences: smells, sounds, tastes, textures. "Holding Whelks and Periwinkles tingling in his hand," for example, conveys both a picture and a sensation of feeling—the reader can see in Donovan's "Starfish-On-The-Toast" an old man holding the sea creatures and can experience vicariously the sensation the old man has of holding something alive and moving. The lines from Judy Collins' "Albatross" communicate an auditory image and a visual image:

> She hears the steeple bells
> Ringing through the orchard
> All the way from town

The use of images enables the poet to convey his ideas more precisely and concretely by increasing the area of contact between himself and his audience, giving them more that they can directly share. The strength of the poetic image lies in its vivid rendering of specific detail, since it is through the specific details that the poet and reader may share the experience. See for example, John Keats' sonnet "Keen, Fitful Gusts Are Whisp'ring Here and There." Keats could have communicated his mood simply by saying, "I didn't mind the long walk home through the cold, dark night because I was full of the happiness I had shared with my friends." To render this experience in poetry, however, Keats employs a wealth of concrete, specific images.

> Keen, fitful gusts are whisp'ring here and there
>> Among the bushes half leafless, and dry;
>> The stars look very cold about the sky,
> And I have many miles on foot to fare.
> Yet feel I little of the cool bleak air,
>> Or of the dead leaves rustling drearily,
>> Or of those silver lamps that burn on high,
> Or of the distance from home's pleasant lair:

For I am brimfull of the friendliness
   That in a little cottage I have found;
Of fair-hair'd Milton's eloquent distress,
   And all his love for gentle Lycid drown'd;
Of lovely Laura in her light green dress,
   And faithful Petrarch gloriously crown'd.

Through these images, the reader is able to leap the gap of time and space (physical as well as psychological) and to share the experience with the poet.

The difference between showing and telling is a matter of degree. To return to our shared garden, if I simply tell you the garden contained red roses, I may not have made you experience their deep crimson color, their velvety texture, their heavy fragrance. The degree to which we both experience my rose will depend on my skill in recreating my rose for you through verbal images that are not only precise and concrete but fresh and original. Another example: "The sky is partly cloudy"— while creating a picture, is not really poetic. "The blue of the sky was broken by slivers of cloud" contains more detail and perhaps has a touch of poetry. "The faded-denim sky" presents an image with a touch of originality and freshness that startles the reader into a new perception. He sees the sky in a way he probably had not previously pictured it—as *like* something else.

To say something is like something else is another aspect of imagery. This is called metaphor, but we'll go on to that in the next section.

1. "Tin Can Alley" describes a poverty stricken, urban tenement scene. "The Tinker and the Crab" describes a beach scene. "The Lullaby of Spring" describes a countryside scene. If images are concrete bridges between the poet and his audience, to what extent are the images in these lyrics bridges for you? What experiences of these scenes can you bring to bear on the language encounter? Would you substitute some of your own images for those in the songs? Why do you think the poet selected only the images he used, from all the possible images that could have been used to describe these scenes?

2. Do you feel that poems succeed better in recreating an experience if they use images that appeal to more than one of the senses? Why (not) ? Is there a connection with "area of shared experience"?

3. Ezra Pound defined an image as "an intellectual and emotional complex united in an instant of time." How much do you feel images contribute to the emotional content of these songs? Lyric poetry has traditionally been the most emotional of poetic forms. Why do you think this is so? Do you think the tradition carries over into the songs of today?

METAPHOR

Aristotle told us in the *Poetics* that metaphor consists of giving something a name that belongs to something else. We can draw at least three important inferences from his statement. First, metaphor, by his definition, seems to be a process and not a device, as it is so often considered. In this section we shall be speaking of metaphor as a process. The word comes from the Greek *metapherein,* which means literally "to carry over"; thus, we can say that metaphor is the process of carrying over.

Second, there seem to be two components involved in the metaphoric process—a "something" and a "something else." I. A. Richards, in *The Philosophy of Rhetoric* (1936), classified the components as "tenor" and "vehicle." The tenor is carried over by the vehicle. In the line "My love is like a red, red rose," "love" is the tenor, and "red, red rose" is the vehicle. We think of all the qualities of the image that the poet presents (especially the emphasized redness), and carry them over to apply to his love. In this instance an abstract condition is communicated by relating it to a concrete image. In every metaphor at least one of the components must be an image, since, as we discussed earlier, these are the concrete bridges that connect our separate minds.

Third, Aristotle mentions the giving of a name. The poet has traditionally been defined as "name-giver." Think of the importance of naming things. Remember Adam creating his own personal order by naming all the creatures and things in his garden. He was naming them in order to know them, in order to give them meaning. Learning the name of a person, or of a complex chemical compound, is a big step over the hurdle of knowing them. Moreover, if things ("things" in the broadest sense of the term, which includes actions, directions, and concepts, as well as concrete objects) had no names, how would we communicate our experiences of them? It would be extremely difficult, not only because we would lack a common language for communicating but also because the things themselves would not be ordered in our minds. To name is to order.

Aristotle also said that metaphor lends style and charm to writing. This comment is the origin of a popular concept of metaphor as an ornamental device in writing and speaking. Within this concept, metaphor stands beside simile, personification, reification, metonymy, and synecdoche as another category of figurative language, as another literary trope. In this sense it is defined simply as "an implied comparison." This concept is perfectly valid and is useful when analyzing poetry. In a broader sense, however, metaphor includes all the above categories. Moreover, it is a process of learning, as well as the principal means by which language lives and grows. Let's take a minute to illustrate these two capacities. When something new comes along, how do we go about learning what it is? We normally examine it to discover any likenesses to the things we do know. From our comparisons we make an association, and (after noting its differences) we draw the newcomer into the fold of our knowledge. Did you ever try to describe a new kind of food to someone? You probably said, "It tastes something like . . . , and it looks something like . . . ." You used metaphor (specifically simile) in order to communicate. As in the metaphor of the red, red rose, you related something the other person didn't know with something he already knew.

After Adam had given out the original names, his descendants used the process of metaphor to fit new names to new experiences, always comparing the new with the old. Hence, the supports of a chair are called "legs," after the supports of a man. Likewise the "arms." The appendages of a clock are called "hands," after those of a man. So with the "eyes" of a potato. A king is called the "head" of state. He is said to be "higher" than his subjects, who look "up" to him. These, a limited sample, are all metaphors, although nowadays we don't think of them as such because they have been absorbed so completely by the language. Indeed they are known as "dead" metaphors (a term which is, of course, another metaphor). But they indicate the process of living language. We assimilate our new experiences by naming them, always using our knowledge of the given language. Fresh and startling metaphors grow old and weary, and as they become a part of our everyday language, we search for new ones to meet our new encounters, thereby ordering them.

Metaphor is a poetic power, and the poet is the chief metaphor-maker. Metaphors synthesize, and it has traditionally been the role of the poet, besides making the metaphors for the ideals of his age, to point with his art toward the unity and harmony of the world. The poet uses metaphors in his poems to intensify description and to make the audience experience in a new way. Thus, Ezra Pound refers to modern civilization as "an old bitch, gone in the teeth." The historian Toynbee warns us that the hydrogen bomb is history's exclamation point. J. Alfred Prufrock, in Eliot's poem, laments that he has measured out his life with coffee spoons. Bob Dylan, in his song "Maggie's Farm," in describing how mean and nasty Maggie's pa is, tells us that his bedroom window is made out of bricks, and adds that the national guard stands outside pa's door. Judy Collins' lady, in the song "Albatross,"

> . . .watches sea gulls fly
> silver on the ocean
> stitching through the waves
> the edges of the sky.

These are all brilliant metaphors (also, note that they are made of brilliant images). They all "carry over" the qualities of one thing to another. They make us see things in another way. They add dimensions of meaning to the poems. Walt Whitman in "Song of Myself" gives us an illustration of the poet as chief metaphor-maker:

> A child said *What is the grass?* fetching it to me with full hands;
> How could I answer the child? I do not know what it is any more
>   than he.

> I guess it must be the flag of my disposition, out of hopeful
>   green stuff woven.
> Or I guess it is the handkerchief of the Lord,
> A scented gift and remembrancer designedly dropt,
> Bearing the owner's name someway in the corners, that we
>   may see and remark, and say *Whose?*

> Or I guess the grass is itself a child, the produced babe of
>   the vegetation.
> Or I guess it is a uniform hieroglyphic,
> And it means, sprouting alike in broad zones and narrow zones,
> Growing among black folks as among white,
> Kanuck, Tuskahoe, Congressman, Cuff, I give them the same, I
>   receive them the same.

> And now it seems to me the beautiful uncut hair of graves.

Whitman's lines demonstrate that the poet also uses metaphors in order to make us see *old* things in new ways, thereby making the old new again for us, enlarging our scope, making us grow.

Sometimes whole poems can be metaphors themselves of the experience the poet wishes to communicate. To use I. A. Richards' terms, the poem is the vehicle, and the tenor is something inside the poet, perhaps something he is not able to state directly. Consider the following poem.

if flowers were the only alive things a rose
would be my mother
my father's stronger boughs
would keep us from all harm
if love were rain drops God
would send a daily shower
to fill a flower's thirst and then be done
and when autumn brings its pose
of somber weather
urging in the breath of winter's storm
i would grow so tall to pierce
the clouds
and pick (for them) a bouquet
of brightness from the sun

In the poem, the poet sustains the images of nature as a vehicle for expressing love, affection and gratitude to his parents. Thus, vehicle + tenor = metaphor.

To summarize: Metaphor is a process of association in language, a way of knowing, a way of naming in terms of what has already been named. The poet is chief metaphor-maker. He uses metaphors in his poems, and sometimes his poems are metaphors themselves.

1. Are there any metaphors used in the songs you have read that you can remember right now? Which were the most unusual analogies? Did you find any in which you could not understand the association between tenor and vehicle?

2. Simile, metaphor, personification, reification, metonymy, synecdoche: Do you know the difference between these kinds of figures? Certain Puritans in Colonial America frowned on metaphor in poetry, although they permitted simile. Why do you think they made the distinction?

3. Metaphors are not limited to noun components. Can you find any metaphors involving verbs, adjectives, or other parts of speech?

4. Can you find any "dead" metaphors in the songs in this book? Any clichés? What about slang expressions? Richard Goldstein in *The Poetry of Rock* has said that slang has the same function in rock lyrics as classical allusions have in written poetry. Do you think the analogy is valid? Do you think slang is an appropriate means of metaphorical expression for rock and folk poetry?

5. Are some poems, as wholes, more metaphorical than others? Is metaphor a matter of degree? Would you accept a thesis that all art is essentially metaphorical in its conception?

SYMBOL

$+$

$+\ +\ +$

Rose

cat

$| + | = 2$

H_2O

All language is symbol. On the most basic level, spoken language exists and functions only because people have agreed that certain combinations of sounds will stand for certain concepts, objects, and ideas. Similarly, written language exists because we have agreed that certain shapes will represent certain sounds. For example, we have agreed that the combination of the shapes "c," "a," and "t" will represent the sound that stands for a small, furry, feline creature.

Symbol functions in all areas of knowledge. Mathematics consists almost entirely of symbols: "1 + 1 = 2" is a purely symbolic statement. The numerals stand for units, the "+" and "=" signs stand for the operation of adding. Similarly, in chemistry the sign "H_2O" represents a certain combination of elements that constitutes water.

Symbolizing is a natural human activity. Over a period of time, some objects come to stand for ideas, as a flag stands for a country, or a rose stands for love. In the same way, actions come to stand for other means for communication. In our culture, when you nod your head, your action is a symbol for agreement. When you shake hands with someone, you are repeating an ancient ritual that stands for goodwill, or at least an indication that you are not going to attack. In fact, our custom of handshaking is a remnant of a time when the act had a very real significance. A man carrying a spear or some other hand weapon actually disarmed himself when he grasped another man's right hand (assuming, of course, that he was right-handed). Since not many of us go around carrying spears any more, the act is now purely symbolic in nature. In essence then, all communication is dependent on symbol.

By a similar process, certain images become symbols; they represent more than simply the objects they refer to. A clear illustration of the steps of symbolization may be seen in the cross. First, the word "cross" is a combination of letters that represents a combination of sounds. These sounds represent a physical object—two sticks or boards fastened together in a certain shape. Since this contraption was used at one time to execute the basest of criminals, the cross became associated with punishment of the most shameful kind. From the Christian standpoint, however, the story of the crucifixion changed the symbolic meaning of the cross. It came to represent, in the Judeo-Christian tradition, the sacrifice made by the Messiah, and thus stands for God's redemptive love. And so it goes with many symbols, with additional levels of meaning being added as experiences change.

The expression used to explain the function of a symbol—that it "stands for" something else—serves as a concrete illustration of the relationship between a symbol and what it represents. The symbol retains its own identity and yet has other identities as well. A marriage by proxy provides a good analogy for this relationship. The person who "stands in" for the missing bride or groom is, for the purposes of the ceremony, that missing person. He remains himself and at the same time is someone else.

In poetry, also, a symbol is something that represents or "stands for" something else. Symbols are images of one kind or another—a river, a garden, a rose, an animal, or a human being, such as the Red Cross Knight in Spenser's *Faerie Queene.* Or the image may be of a different type—an action, such as dancing, or a sound, such as music. Although a symbol is always an image, an image is not always a symbol. A poet can elect, however, to make any image in his poetry a symbol. In other words, he can create an image that refers to more than an object or a sensory experience; it refers to or stands for something else in addition to the image that it evokes. The transition from image to symbol involves the addition of layers of meaning. Symbol involves more than comparison, more than the implication that "something" is *like* "something else." As in the wedding by proxy, that "something" *is* "something else." Simultaneously. On many levels, according to context.

It is at this point, then, that symbol differs from metaphor. The process of metaphor is basically the process of comparison, of showing how something is like something else. The relationship between the symbol and the thing it stands for is much closer than likeness. The two things are actually intertwined—the symbol is the other thing(s).

Consider the song "Spanish Harlem" in terms of our discussion this far. The rose of Spanish Harlem is an image; it refers to a concrete object we can experience through our senses. In addition, the rose is a metaphor for a girl; the girl is like a rose. The rose-girl metaphor functions throughout the language of the poem. The speaker wants to pick the rose—marry the girl—and watch it grow in his garden—watch her flourish in the environment he will create for her. Outside of the context of any particular poem, however, the rose exists in its own right as a symbol of love, of beauty, of queenliness, of sweetness, of purity. Thus the poet, in comparing the girl to a rose, is able to draw on the general symbolic properties of roses, and thereby add another dimension to his poem. William Blake, in "The Sick Rose," also utilizes the symbolic properties we associate with roses to deepen the experience of his poem. The destruction of all the beautiful qualities roses suggest makes the destruction of this particular rose even more appalling, and more significant.

Precisely what symbolic associations the rose carries will depend at least to some extent on the things a rose represents to the individual reader, and here we encounter one of the differences between ordinary symbols and literary symbols. The symbols we talked about earlier—letters, signs, the cross—all have certain designated meanings that those of us who share the same culture and traditions recognize. A plus sign always means the same thing. In poetry, however, the meaning of the symbol may vary according to the context of the work and according to the meaning(s) the reader derives from the work. A poetic symbol may not have any one precise meaning; there may be no "right answer" to the question of what it represents. Indeed, the most successful poetic symbols stand for many meanings, so that through symbol a poem becomes infinitely richer and more complex.

We may further distinguish between kinds of poetic symbols by differentiating between arbitrary and natural symbols. To make an arbitrary symbol, the poet selects an image to stand for his meaning, and there may be little intrinsic relationship between the image and the thing it symbolizes. For example, a minus sign contains nothing within itself that in any way corresponds to the operation of subtraction. The sign has been arbitrarily designated to represent the operation. Similarly, in "The Hind and the Panther," Dryden's hind and panther stand for the Protestant and Catholic churches, but there is nothing within a panther or deer that automatically suggests the symbolic meaning with which Dryden endows them. John Donne's poem "The Flea" illustrates the way in which a poet may select as symbol an image that has little direct relationship to the thing it stands for. Donne employs the unlikely image of a flea to symbolize the relationship between the lovers:

Mark but this flea, and mark in this,
How little that which thou deny'st me is;
It sucked me first, and now sucks thee,
And in this flea, our two bloods mingled be;
Thou know'st that this cannot be said
A sin, nor shame, nor loss of maidenhead,
    Yet this enjoys before it woo,
      And pampered swells with one blood made
        of two,
    And this, alas, is more than we would do.

Oh, stay, three lives in one flea spare,
where we almost, yea more than married are.
This flea is you and I, and this
Our marriage bed, and marriage temple is;
Though parents grudge, and you, we are met
And cloistered in these living walls of jet.
    Though use make you apt to kill me,
    Let not, to that, self murder added be,
    And sacrilege, three sins in killing three.

Cruel and sudden, has thou since
Purpled thy nail, in blood of innocence?
Wherein could this flea guilty be,
Except in that drop which it sucked from thee?
Yet thou triumph'st and say'st that thou
Find'st not thy self, nor me the weaker now;
   'Tis true, then learn how false fears be;
   Just so much honor, when thou yield'st to me,
   Will waste, as this flea's death took life from thee.

When we consider the way in which the flea functions as a symbol in this poem, we are in a position to gain some insights into the nature of symbol. The blood of the lovers intermingles in the flea; by drawing sustenance from each, the flea incorporates their lives into his (blood operating here as a symbol of life) and thus the three lives become one. Yet the flea retains its own identity—it remains a flea, which is certainly a distasteful creature. At the same time, however, the lovers are now joined within the flea, which thus functions both as a concrete image and as a symbol for an abstract relationship.

Donne's flea is an arbitrary symbol, elaborately and ingeniously constructed from two basically dissimilar things. A natural symbol, however, has a different kind of relationship with the thing it represents. A natural symbol already contains within itself something of the qualities it stands for. Donovan's "The Lullaby of Spring" abounds with natural symbols. Images of plants and flowers unfolding from the rich earth, wet and windy skies, birds and animals giving birth all merge in the dominant image of spring. Since all of these images picture the process of birth and rebirth, the entire song represents an image of life's eternal birth-death-rebirth cycle. The linking of the physical life cycle with the image of the easter bells ringing in the village church makes these images symbolic of the spiritual concept of birth-death-rebirth embodied in the Christian tradition. Besides being images drawn from nature, these images are natural symbols—they contain within themselves the qualities they stand for.

The terms "natural symbols" and "nature symbols" should not be confused, however. The term "natural symbol" does not refer specifically to symbols drawn from nature but rather it explains an intrinsic similarity between the symbol and the thing it stands for. Of course, many natural symbols may be discovered in nature images, as the Donovan song illustrates. However, natural symbols occur in other planes of experience as well. Dante's use of his love for Beatrice as a symbol of the love between man and God is one striking example. In a similar fashion, music makes an excellent natural symbol for harmony and order because it consists of harmonies in an orderly arrangement. The image of the dancer provides another example. Consider the relationship between the dancer and the dance. The dance has a concrete existence only when someone is dancing. We can see and experience the dance only when watching someone perform a dance, or when we are dancing ourselves. Similarly, the dancer exists *as a dancer* only when engaged in the physical activity of the dance. The two are inextricably tied together and thus join to form an image which then becomes a natural symbol for unity.

To summarize: symbolizing is a natural human activity. Many of our daily objects and actions are symbols. Indeed, the nature of human language itself is symbolic. In poetry, images become symbols when they acquire meaning beyond that which they denote. When an image is itself and yet stands for something else (or many other things) it is a symbol. Metaphors indicate likeness; symbols indicate fusion. Distinctions can be made between ordinary and poetic symbols, between arbitrary and natural symbols, and between natural and nature symbols.

1. Can you find examples of natural symbols and arbitrary symbols in the songs?

2. The symbolic connotation of flowers is a contemporary example of the way in which a symbol may acquire additional levels of meaning. How are flowers used in the songs? How many levels of meaning can you discover?

3. There is a considerable amount of color symbolism employed in the songs in this text. Make a comparative study of the way colors are used in the songs as image, metaphor, and symbol.

4. Can you find evidences of symbolic actions in the songs?

5. Are symbols wherever you find them? Is everything "symbolic," depending on your ability to see symbolism? Take every image in a poem and show it

could be a symbol of something. Beat it to death. Overkill the method of symbolic approach. Compare your results with those of others in your class. Do you think there might be any dangers in this kind of "symbol hunting"?

6. Is the act of singing symbolic? Are songs themselves symbols? In his novel, *Dr. Zhivago,* Boris Pasternak said that a song is "an insane attempt to stop time by means of its words." How does this definition relate to the above two questions?

MYTH AND ARCHETYPE

Since earliest history began, man has attempted to understand and explain the world he lives in. Long before written literature, long before scientific methods of observing and interpreting were developed, men confronted the chaos of experience by devising stories to explain the bewildering events that surrounded them. What is the sun, and where does it go at night? What causes thunder and lightning and rain? Why does a season change from being warm and sunny and full of vegetation to a dark, cold period when many living things die? Where do the new plants come from in the spring? Where did the first man come from? Or, for that matter, the earth itself?

In trying to answer these puzzling and often frightening questions, men developed elaborate stories. Naturally enough, these stories were constructed mostly from the images that people were most familiar with, and so stories grew around supernatural figures who were remarkably like the men who made them. They fought, laughed, and made love. They created people by molding clay images and breathing life into them. They caused lightning by hurling fiery bolts across the sky. When they became angry, they churned the waves into tempests and blew great gusts of wind from their mouths.

By this process, men created myths, explaining their origins and their environment, bringing order to the chaos that surrounded them by interpreting the unknown in terms of the known. Myth, then, functions in very much the same way as metaphor, by comparison and analogy, and for very much the same reasons; that is, myth-making is basically an ordering process. We can probably say, generally, that myth is metaphor with a narrative framework.

Characters and events will of course vary in different cultures, according to the times and to the environments, but each society evolves a mythology. Our cultural tradition blends several bodies of myth—biblical, Greek, Roman, and Norse, to name the principal older ones, whose remnants linger in our language in the names of the days and months, and in countless idiomatic expressions. But although we tend to think of mythmaking as the product of a primitive time, it is actually, like metaphor, a continuous process. The American people have created a mythology based partly on historical and legendary events, partly on the character and spirit of the country. The myths of the frontier, the old West, and the antebellum South feature a mixture of real and fictional persons, such as Paul Bunyan and Paul Revere, Davy Crockett and Buffalo Bill, Scarlet O'Hara and Betsy Ross (you can see from the examples that myth is being used here in its broadest sense, encompassing such categories as history, legend, fable, and fiction).

Myth has always played a prominent role in literature. Indeed, the Bible, the *Iliad* and *Odyssey,* and the *Aeneid,* some of our earliest collections of myths, remain today among the greatest of literary works. Throughout the history of literature, great writers such as Shakespeare, Dante, and Milton not only dwelt on mythological themes, but also constantly employed mythological allusions in their poetry in order to enrich the meaning by association. Modern writers have a wealth of mythical material to work with. Some, like James Joyce in *Ulysses,* use old myths in new settings and in new perspectives; others, like T. S. Eliot in the *Wasteland,* draw on a variety of mythical traditions; a few, like W. B. Yeats, utilizing material eclectically from a myriad of sources, go on to create their own personal mythology. The modern writer, like his forbears, uses mythological allusions as a kind of shorthand, as a method by which he can invest his work with the added dimension of an entire body of mythical associations. Thus Eliot by simply referring to Agamemnon in "Sweeney Among the Nightingales," and Yeats in merely mentioning Leda in "Among School Children," are able to conjure up the whole epic cycle of the Trojan War.

Songwriter-poets today continue in the poetic tradition of drawing on myth to add richer meaning to their works. Donovan's "Atlantis" recognizes the seeds of the legendary lost community in our own society. John Phillips, in "California Dreamin'," reinvokes the frontier optimism of the westward drive to California while aiming at its current mythical-utopian associations. Lennon-McCartney's "The Continuing Story of Bungalow Bill" provides an ironic twist of the Buffalo Bill stories.

To conclude, the poet as mythmaker is related to the poet as metaphor-maker. That is, he employs myth (whether traditional or of his own creation) to render concrete the intangible, to bring order out of confusion.

As we have noted in the discussion on symbol, natural phenomena provide many images that serve as symbols. Because all men, whatever their culture and traditions, share the basic experience of the natural physical world we live in (for examples, the sun passes overhead daily, the seasons die and renew themselves, all human bodies have the same physiological processes, all male bodies have the same basic anatomy, as do all female bodies), certain images drawn from this shared experience recur, in similar patterns, in the various mythologies, folk tales, literature, and other means of creative language expression. The sun as the source of life, the sea as a death-rebirth symbol, male phallic symbols such as trees, spears, etc., female womb symbols such as bowls and containers—these are only a few of the images that have been employed as poetic symbols from the most primitive myths to the most current and sophisticated literary works. These symbols are called "archetypal" symbols.

Experts who have done comparative studies of individual myths, folktales, and literary works have found that they share, besides these common natural symbols, common basic types of characters, places (situations), and events. These basic types also appeared in the earliest myths, and have recurred in similar patterns throughout the history of storytelling. These also are referred to as "archetypes." The word means literally the first or chief form. An archetype can thus be considered either as the original model from which all subsequent images, characters, places, and events followed, or as the general, unifying category under which the accidental varieties fall.

We have already mentioned some images that are literary archetypes. Some examples of archetypal characters are: the hero, the fool, the wanderer, the enchantress, the mysterious stranger, the devil, the wise old man. Some archetypal places are: the garden, the happy island, the mountain, the battlefield, the cave, the dungeon. Some archetypal events are: the fall (as from paradise, or from the innocence of childhood), the death-rebirth pattern, the quest (as for the father, or for the holy grail), the return, the contest (as between generations, or rivalry among brothers), the descent into hell.

These examples are among the many that are common to the one big story of mankind. You probably are having no trouble immediately identifying the existence of each one in several poems, songs, stories, films, or even television programs you are familiar with. Their constant appearance in all these media constitutes one collective demonstration of the shared experience that unites us all.

Any critical approach to literature that considers archetypes is predicated on a belief in this commonality. Around the turn of the century, research in two different fields combined to produce an awareness of such an archetypal theory that could be applied to literature. Studies in comparative anthropology, most notably that of Sir James Frazer, and Carl Jung's studies in depth psychology produced significant archetypal theories. There have been a few different approaches to the origin of the archetypal experience, centering around the question of just wherein does this commonality exist. As we noted earlier, what men (and women) have in common physiologically becomes the source of archetypes. Frazer added that certain ideas and experiences were developed into set patterns early in our history by ritual, customs, etc., and they are now so entrenched in human culture that we inherit the whole set culturally. Jung said that in back of the individual's conscious mind is his unconscious, the blocked-off memory of the experiences of the race (or, as Jung termed it, the "psychic residue" of these experiences). This part of the individual's mind he shares with a part of every other individual's mind, and thus, the commonality. The archetype is the key that unlocks this unconscious, racial memory vault. This part of the mind's response to archetypes is immediate, prelogical, and emotionally powerful.

Archetypes are used intentionally and unintentionally by poets; but the poet who is aware of and uses them possesses a powerful weapon, since he can evoke at will unconscious responses from a stirred racial memory (and/or from an implicit cultural heritage, and/or from a common bond of physiological perceptions). The poet who uses archetypes speaks in a voice that is stronger than his own. He lifts the purely personal experience into the universal racial experience; he extends the transitory to the eternal.

The following are just a few of the songs in this book that use archetypes: "Moonchild" uses archetypal natural symbols—the sun and the moon—to depict the relationship between the sexual encounter, the rebirth pattern, and the daily cycle. "People Are Strange" comments on the plight of the wanderer. "The Lullaby of Spring" uses the archetypal season of rebirth. "Penny Lane" is a description of paradise.

1. Make your own lists of characters, things, places, and events that you would consider archetypal (consult the reading list in the back of the book for some references that will help you expand your knowledge in this area). Compare your lists to those of others in the class. Make a comprehensive list. Now, look for archetypal patterns in and outside of literature. Does this awareness give you a different perspective on particular events?

2. There is a great deal to be done with myth, if you are interested. You might, for example, want to compare how the same archetypes are given different treatment in the various mythical stories of different countries. Or, you might try to ascertain any new and current American myths.

CONCLUSION

Statement, image, metaphor, symbol, myth, and archetype—levels of the "meaning" of poetry. Some poets manipulate all of these levels in a single poem, taking their audience on a journey through the heights and depths of the human condition. In such cases the poem joins not only poet with audience, but also poet and audience with the common experience that we have called "archetypal." It would perhaps be beneficial at this time to briefly examine two poems that reach all of these dimensions of poetic meaning. Our purpose will be to synthesize the things we've discussed in sequence in this chapter.

The first is William Blake's "The Sick Rose," included here on p. 43. This short poem consists of two sentences in which the speaker addresses a rose, announcing its sickness and impending death, which is being caused by a worm. This is the poem's literal statement, and it suffices for a first reading. The images in the poem, however, intensify the horror of the destruction. The worm is invisible, and he flies in the night, in howling storms. Opposing these images of terror is the rose's "bed of crimson joy." The images have concretized and individualized the rose and the worm.

Blake makes much use of metaphor and symbol. Both rose and worm are personified. The destruction of the rose is likened to a sexual encounter. And, as we discover additional layers of meaning, we may conclude that the poem itself is a metaphorical expression or the vehicle for some undefined tenor within the poet's mind. We mentioned earlier that the rose is a natural symbol of beauty, purity, and love; it is also symbolic of the female. The worm is a natural phallic symbol and it also symbolizes the lower aspect of love—lust. Thus, the poem can be read (on one level) as the symbolic destruction of love by lust.

We also associate the worm (via the snake) with vileness and deceit, and this is largely a result of the biblical account of the Garden of Eden. In fact, the myth is reenacted in Blake's poem. The rose is associated (by metonymy) with the garden, and the worm, of course, is the serpent. The archetypal event enacted in the Garden of Eden is the fall, in this case the fall of man from innocence, from God's grace.

Thus, our examination of Blake's ostensibly simple poem has revealed several strata of meaning. Let's try the same procedure with another poem, this time one of the song lyrics—Carl Oglesby's "Black Panther" printed here on p. 106. A first reading of the poem finds an impressionistic narrative in which the speaker is saying "I told you so" to a woman who has been attacked by a panther, because she did not heed the speaker's warnings that the panther exists and had found her "perfume trail." This is the basic literal statement, but it is difficult to remain on this level very long, because the images Oglesby offers us cry out for inspection. For example, he blends images of some kind of decadent aristocratic setting (Japanese umbrella, cocktail party conversation, garden and vineyard, footman, coach, swing, etc.) with images of religion and prophecy (Jesus, *I Ching,* dime horoscope).

Metaphors and symbols abound in the poem. "Lollipop eyes" is a single metaphor that effectively communicates something about the woman's personality as well as describing her physical features. The sixth stanza of the poem consists of several metaphors either of the woman's mind or her seemingly protected environment. Moreover, we can also conceive of the poem itself as a metaphor, the story, as in "The Sick Rose," becoming a kind of allegory. There are several kinds of symbols in the poem. Trees, knives, the stallion, and the ram are masculine symbols. The Japanese umbrella symbolizes the flimsy, gaudy, and artificial protection the woman has from reality. The "virgo down on the ram" is a symbolic portent of what will happen to her. The panther itself suggests several possible associations, from the racial-revolutionary cultural context to the archetypal meeting with death.

The story enacted here is also related to the biblical account of Eden and the archetypal fall. The woman is Eve. The paradise she has shut herself up in is the already ruined paradise of pleasure in a decadent aristocratic society (gardens and roses in the song allude to the mythical garden). She refuses to acknowledge the reality of evil, or the evil of reality. Her fall is from an innocence that has already withered.

Our discussion of these two poems does not even approach their full meaning and significance; the discussion was merely meant to uncover the various ways in which they do mean. Good poems should be probed, and can be probed many times with each time discovering something new. Our focus in this chapter has been on the dimensions of the poetic experience. We have talked about ways of approaching a poem on all its levels. These approaches can be applied to good poems anywhere, from ancient to modern, from epic to lyric. And there are good poems. Everywhere. On the air waves. Right now.

Supplemental Readings

The following is intended as a supplemental reading list for students who want to penetrate further into the areas the book has covered . . . or uncovered, as the case may be. It is divided into two parts. The first part lists publications (either scholarship or collections of lyrics) that are related to those topics raised in Chapter I—the evolution of lyric form, cultural influences on the lyric, and the contemporary lyric scene. The list directs the student to sources that will fill in some of the gaps and expand some of the ideas that were consolidated in Chapter I in order to maintain a clear and simple introduction. Some of the more obvious and easily attainable references, such as to Blake's poems, are not included.

The second part lists works that conduct further investigations into the areas related to Chapter V—"Discussions on Poetic Meaning."

The entries in each section are in alphabetical order, by the author's (or editor's) name. As a rule, we have not listed books that have already been cited in the text Chapters II, III, and IV.

PART I. Works Related to Chapter I
The evolution of lyric form, cultural influences on the lyric, and the contemporary lyric scene

Amaya, Mario. *Pop Art . . . and After.* 1965.
Auden, W. H., and C. Kallman, ed. *Elizabethan Song Book.* 1957.
Balakian, Anna. *The Symbolist Movement.* 1967.
Belz, Carl. *The Story of Rock.* 1969.
Boas, Frederick S. , ed. *Songs and Lyrics from the English Playbooks.* 1945.
Bowra, Cecil M. *Primitive Song.* 1962.
Bullen, Arthur Henry, ed. *Lyrics from the Songbooks of the Elizabethan Age.* 1897.
Burn, Andrew R. *The Lyric Age of Greece.* 1960.
Caws, Mary Ann. *Surrealism and the Literary Imagination.* 1966.
Chambers, E. K. *Early English Lyrics.* 1926.

190

Charters, Samuel B. *The Country Blues.* 1959.

Chiari, Joseph. *Symbolism from Poe to Mallarmé.* 1956.

Child, Francis James. *English and Scottish Popular Ballads.* 1932.

Clinton-Baddeley, V. C. *Words for Music.* 1941.

Cohen, John M. *The Baroque Lyric.* 1963.

Cohn, Nik. *Rock from the Beginning.* 1969.

Creekmore, Hubert. *Lyrics of the Middle Ages.* 1959.

DeTurk, David A. and A. Poulin, Jr. eds. *The American Folk Scene: Dimensions of the Folksong Revival.* 1967.

Drinkwater, John. *The Lyric.* 1915.

Dronke, Peter. *The Medieval Lyric.* 1968.

Duncan, Edmonstoune. *Story of Minstrelsy.* 1907.

Eisen, Jonathan, ed. *The Age of Rock: Sounds of the American Cultural Revolution.* 1969.

_____. *The Age of Rock, Two: Sounds of the American Cultural Revolution.* 1970.

Eliot, T. S. *On Poetry and Poets.* 1957.

Erskine, John. *The Elizabethan Lyric.* 1903.

Fowlie, Wallace. *Age of Surrealism.* 1950.

Friedman, Albert B. *The Ballad Revival: Studies in the Influence of Popular on Sophisticated Poetry.* 1961.

Frye, Northrop, ed. *Sound and Poetry.* 1957.

Gerould, Gordon H. *The Ballad of Tradition.* 1957.

Gershman, Herbert S. *The Surrealist Revolution in France.* 1969.

Gibbon, John Murray. *Melody and the Lyric from Chaucer to the Cavaliers.* 1964.

Ginsberg, Allen. "Some Metamorphoses of Personal Prosody," in *Naked Poetry,* ed. Stephen Berg and Robert Mezey. 1969. pp. 221-222.

Goldstein, Richard, ed. *The Poetry of Rock.* 1968.

Grierson, Herbert J. C. *Lyrical Poetry from Blake to Hardy.* 1928.

Gummere, Francis B. *The Beginnings of Poetry.* 1901.

_____. *The Popular Ballad.* 1904, 1907.

Henderson, T. F. *The Ballad in Literature.* 1912.

Hollander, J. *Untuning the Sky: Ideas of Music in English Poetry, 1500–1700.* 1960.

Ivey, Donald. *Song: Anatomy, Imagery and Style.* 1970.

Jones, Leroi. *Blues People: Negro Music in White America.* 1963.

Kar, Gangascharan. *Thoughts on the Medieval Lyric.* 1933.

Kastandiek, Miles M. *England's Musical Poet, Thomas Campion.* 1938.

Keil, Charles. *Urban Blues.* 1966.

Lewis, C. Day. *The Lyric Impulse.* 1965.

Lomax, John A. , comp. *American Ballads and Folk Songs.* 1935.

———. *Our Singing Country: A Second Volume of American Ballads and Folk Songs.* 1941.

Lucie-Smith, Edward, ed. *The Liverpool Scene: Pop Poetry and Interviews Recorded Live Along the Merzey Beat.* 1968.

Mallarmé, Stephane. *Selected Prose Poems, Essays and Letters,* trans. Bradford Cook. 1956.

Matthews, J. H. *An Introduction to Surrealism.* 1965.

McLuhan, Herbert Marshall. *The Gutenberg Galaxy.* 1962.

———. *Understanding Media.* 1964.

McLuhan, Herbert Marshall and Quentin Fiore. *War and Peace in the Global Village.* 1968.

Meltzer, Richard. *The Aesthetics of Rock.* 1970.

Nelson, Lowry. *Baroque Lyric Poetry.* 1961.

Nettel, Reginald. *Seven Centuries of Popular Song.* 1956.

Nettl, Bruno. *Music in Primitive Culture.* 1956.

Northcote, Syden. *The Ballad in Music.* 1942.

Oliver, Paul. *Blues Fell This Morning.* 1960.

Parkinson, Thomas F., ed. *A Casebook on the Beat.* 1961.

Pattison, Bruce. *Music and Poetry of the English Renaissance.* 1948.

Pearce, Roy Harvey. *The Continuity of American Poetry.* 1961.

Pound, Louis. *Poetic Origins and the Ballad.* 1962.

Raymond, George Lansing. *Rhythm and Harmony in Poetry and Music.* 1909.

Rhys, Ernest. *Lyric Poetry.* 1913.

Rublowsky, John. *Pop Art.* 1965.

Sachs, Curt. *The Rise of Music in the Ancient World.* 1943.

Sackheim, Eric, comp. *The Blues Line: A Collection of Blues Lyrics.* 1969.

Schelling, Felix. *The English Lyric.* 1913.

Schmittroth, John, and John Mahoney, eds. *New Poets, New Music.* 1970.

Sears, Minnie Earl. *Song Index.* 1934, 1966.

Sewell, Elizabeth. *The Orphic Voice.* 1960.

Shepard, Leslie. *The Broadside Ballad: A Study in Origins and Meanings.* 1962.

Simpson, Claude M. *The British Broadside Ballad and Its Music.* 1966.

Solt, Mary Ellen, ed. *Concrete Poetry: A World View.* 1968.

Spaeth, Sigmund. *History of Popular Music.* 1948.

Spinner, Stephanie, ed. *Rock Is Beautiful: An Anthology of American Lyrics, 1953–1968.* 1970.

Stevens, Denis W., ed. *A History of Song.* 1960.

Symons, Arthur. *The Symbolist Movement in Literature.* 1919.

Valéry, Paul. *The Art of Poetry,* trans. Denis Folliot. 1958.

Wheeler, A. L. *Catullus and the Traditions of Ancient Poetry.* 1934.

Whimster, Donald Cameron, ed. *A Century of Lyrics, 1550–1650.* 1938.

Wilentz, Elias, and Fred McDarrah. *The Beat Scene.* 1960.

PART II. Works Related to Chapter V
Discussions on Poetic Meaning

Aristotle. *Works,* ed. W. D. Ross, XI (*Rhetoric,* trans. W. Rhys Roberts; *Poetics,* trans. I. Bywater). 1924.
Barfield, Owen. *Poetic Diction.* 1928.
Beebe, Maurice, ed. *Literary Symbolism: An Introduction to the Interpretation of Literature.* 1960.
Bodkin, Maude. *Archetypal Patterns in Poetry.* 1934.
Bowra, Cecil M. *The Heritage of Symbolism.* 1943.
Brooke-Rose, Christine. *A Grammar of Metaphor.* 1958.
Brown, Stephen J. *The World of Imagery.* 1927.
Bryson, L., ed. *Symbols and Values.* 1954.
_____. *Symbols and Society.* 1955.
Buck, G. *The Metaphor: A Study in the Psychology of Rhetoric.* 1899.
Burke, Kenneth. *The Philosophy of Literary Form: Studies in Symbolic Action.* 1941.
Campbell, Joseph. *The Hero with a Thousand Faces.* 1949.
Cassirir, Ernest. *Language and Myth,* trans. S. K. Langer. 1946.
Chase, Richard. *Quest for Myth.* 1949.
Embler, Weller. *Metaphor and Meaning.* 1966.
Foss, Martin. *Symbol and Metaphor in Human Experience.* 1949.
Frye, Northrop. "Levels of Meaning in Literature," *Kenyon Review,* 12 (1950).
_____. "The Archetypes of Literature," *Kenyon Review,* 13 (1950).
Frazer, Sir James George. *The Golden Bough.* 1935.
Hester, Marcus B. *The Meaning of Poetic Metaphor.* 1967.
Jennings, J. G. *An Essay on Metaphor in Poetry.* 1915.
Jung, Carl G. *Man and His Symbols.* 1964.
_____. "The Problem of Types in Poetry," *Psychological Types,* trans. H. G. Baynes. 1923.
Knights, L. C. and Basil Cottle, eds. *Metaphor and Symbol.* 1960.
Lewis, C. Day. *The Poetic Image.* 1947.
May, Rollo, ed. *Symbolism in Religion and Literature.* 1960.
Murray, Henry A., ed. *Myth and Mythmaking.* 1960.
Musurillo, H. *Symbol and Myth in Ancient Poetry.* 1961.
Norman, Dorothy. *The Hero: Myth, Image, Symbol.* 1969.
Preminger, Alex, ed. *Encyclopedia of Poetry and Poetics.* 1965.
Prescott, Frederick C. *Poetry and Myth.* 1927.
Richards, I. A. *The Philosophy of Rhetoric.* 1936.
Seward, Barbara. *The Symbolic Rose.* 1960.
Slote, Bernice, ed. *Myth and Symbol.* 1963.
Tindall, William York. *The Literary Symbol.* 1955.
Turbayne, Colin M. *The Myth of the Metaphor.* 1962.
Vickery, John B., ed. *Myth and Literature.* 1966.

Weathers, Winston. *The Archetype and the Psyche.* 1968.
Wells, Henry W. *Poetic Imagery.* 1924.
Whalley, George. *Poetic Process.* 1953.
Wheelright, Phillip. *Metaphor and Reality.* 1962.

Discography

The following discography also has two parts. The first lists each lyric by title in the order in which it appears in the text, giving also the title of the album from which it is taken, the recording artist, and the record label. The purpose is to direct students toward the performed song, which should be heard, if possible, in order to have the full experience of the art form. The second part is a supplementary list of current recorded poetry in song. The list is representative, but by no means comprehensive. It gives in alphabetical order the name of the artist, the albums that are most representative of high quality lyric poetry, and their labels. Albums included in Part I are not mentioned in Part II. Of course, the individual tastes and judgments of the authors of this text have helped to shape this list, and, again, it is meant only for a guideline, a place to begin. Please add your own choices to it.

PART I.
Lyrics included in Chapter II

"Widow with Shawl"   *Gift from a Flower to a Garden,*
                                          Part II, For Little Ones.
                                          Donovan
                                          Epic

"Sad-Eyed Lady of the Lowlands"   *Blonde on Blonde*
                                          Bob Dylan
                                          Columbia

"As Tears Go By"   *December's Children*
                                          The Rolling Stones
                                          London

"People Are Strange"   *Strange Days*
                                          The Doors
                                          Elektra

"Hey, That's No Way to Say Goodbye" *Songs of Leonard Cohen*
Leonard Cohen
Columbia

"How Long" *Tim Hardin*
Tim Hardin
MGM

"Spoonful" A) *I Am the Blues*
Willie Dixon
Columbia
B) *Wheels of Fire*
Cream
Atco
C) *Ten years After*
Ten Years After
Deram
D) *Blues Project (Live at the
Cafe Au Go-Go)*
Blues Project
Verve
E) *What's Shakin'*
Paul Butterfield
Elektra
F) *Dirty Blues Band*
Dirty Blues Band
Bluesway
G) *I Can Tell*
John Hammond
Atco
H) *Howlin' Wolf*
Howlin' Wolf
Cadet Concept

"I Give You the Morning" *The Things I Notice Now*
Tom Paxton
Elektra

"Moonchild" *In the Court of the Crimson King*
King Crimson
Atco

"Celebration for a Grey Day" *Celebrations for a Grey Day*
Richard & Mimi Fariña
Vanguard

"Since You've Asked"

Wildflowers
Judy Collins
Elektra

"Supergirl"

The Fugs' First Album
The Fugs
Esp

"Spanish Harlem"

Spanish Harlem
Ben E. King
Atco

"Sally, Go 'Round the Roses"

Originally recorded by the Jaynettes; record no longer available except from specialized dealers. A good recording is
Basket of Light
Pentangle
Reprise

"Miss Lonely (Are You Blue?)"

More Hits from Tin Can Alley
Eric Anderson
Vanguard

"If I Were a Carpenter"

Tim Hardin Volume II
Tim Hardin
Verve-Forecast

"Albatross"

Wildflowers
Judy Collins
Elektra

"Dragon Song"

Carl Oglesby
Carl Oglesby
Vanguard

Lyrics included in Chapter III

"The Story of Isaac"

Songs from a Room
Leonard Cohen
Columbia

"Where Have All the Flowers Gone"

Pete Seeger's Greatest Hits
Pete Seeger
Columbia

"The Continuing Story of Bungalow Bill"

The Beatles
The Beatles
Apple

"The Klan"	*Something Else Again* Richie Havens Verve-Forecast
"For What It's Worth"	*Buffalo Springfield* Buffalo Springfield Atco
"Now That the Buffalo's Gone"	*It's My Way* Buffy Sainte-Marie Vanguard
"My Country 'Tis of Thy People You're Dying"	*Little Wheel, Spin and Spin* Buffy Sainte-Marie Vanguard
"Tin Can Alley"	*More Hits from Tin Can Alley* Eric Anderson Vanguard
"Stories of the Street"	*Songs of Leonard Cohen* Leonard Cohen Columbia
"The Gates of Eden"	*Bringing It All Back Home* Bob Dylan Columbia
"Nobody's Buying Flowers from the Flower Lady"	*Pleasures of the Harbor* Phil Ochs A & M
"All Along the Watchtower"	*John Wesley Harding* Bob Dylan Columbia
"Portrait of a Lady"	*Carl Oglesby* Carl Oglesby Vanguard
"Suburbs of Eden"	*Carl Oglesby* Carl Oglesby Vanguard
"Twelve Thirty (Young Girls Are Coming to the Canyon)"	*Farewell to the First Golden Era* The Mamas and the Papas Dunhill

"Atlantis"

Barabajagal
Donovan
Epic

"The End"

The Doors
The Doors
Elektra

"Black Panther"

Carl Oglesby
Carl Oglesby
Vanguard

"The Sound of Silence"

Sounds of Silence
Simon and Garfunkel
Columbia

"Penny Lane"

Magical Mystery Tour
The Beatles
Capitol

Lyrics included in Chapter IV

"Paint It Black"

Aftermath
The Rolling Stones
London

"Blackbird"

The Beatles
The Beatles
Apple

"A Whiter Shade of Pale"

Procol Harum
Procol Harum
Deram

"White Rabbit"

Surrealistic Pillow
Jefferson Airplane
Victor

"The Butcher"

Songs from a Room
Leonard Cohen
Columbia

"The Stranger Song"

Songs of Leonard Cohen
Leonard Cohen
Columbia

"Crucifixion"

Pleasures of the Harbor
Phil Ochs
A & M

"Suzanne"	*Songs of Leonard Cohen* Leonard Cohen Columbia
"California Dreamin' "	*Farewell to the First Golden Era* The Mamas and the Papas Dunhill
"Bird on the Wire"	*Songs from a Room* Leonard Cohen Columbia
"October Song"	*The Incredible String Band* The Incredible String Band Elektra
"Wear Your Love Like Heaven"	*Gift from a Flower to a Garden* *Part I—Wear Your Love Like Heaven* Donovan Epic
"The Tinker and the Crab"	*Gift from a Flower to a Garden* *Part II-For Little Ones* Donovan Epics
"Starfish on the Toast"	*Gift from a Flower to a Garden* *Part II—For Little Ones* Donovan Epic
"The Lullaby of Spring"	*Gift from a Flower to a Garden* *Part II—For Little Ones* Donovan Epic
"Isle of Islay"	*Gift from a Flower to a Garden* *Part II—For Little Ones* Donovan Epic
"Hampstead Incident"	*Mellow Yellow* Donovan Epic
"Koeeoaddi There"	*The Hangman's Beautiful Daughter* The Incredible String Band Elektra

PART II
A Supplemental List of Recorded Poetry in Song

Eric Anderson	*Avalanche*	Warner Bros.
	'Bout Changes 'n Things	Vanguard
	Country Dream	Vanguard
	Today Is the Highway	Vanguard
The Band	*Music from Big Pink*	Capitol
The Beatles	*Abbey Road*	Apple
	Hey Jude	Apple
	Let It Be	Apple
	Revolver	Capitol
	Rubber Soul	Capitol
	Sergeant Pepper's Lonely Hearts Club Band	Capitol
	Yesterday and Today	Capitol
Jaime Brockett	*Jaime Brockett*	Capitol
Tim Buckley	*Blue Afternoon*	Warner Bros.
	Goodbye and Hello	Elektra
	Happy/Sad	Elektra
	Lorca	Elektra
	Starsailor	Warner Bros.
	Tim Buckley	Elektra
Captain Beefheart and His Magic Band	*Lick My Decals Off Baby*	Reprise
	Safe as Milk	Buddah
	Strictly Personal	Blue Thumb
	Trout Mask Replica	Reprise
Country Joe and the Fish	*Electric Music for the Mind and Body*	Vanguard
	I Feel Like I'm Fixing to Die	Vanguard
Cream	*Disraeli Gears*	Atco
Crosby, Stills, And Nash	*Crosby, Stills and Nash*	Reprise
Donovan	*Catch the Wind*	Hickory
	Fairy Tale	Hickory
	Hurdy Gurdy Man	Epic
	Like It Is	Hickory
	Open Road	Epic
	Sunshine Superman	Epic

Doors	Morrison Hotel	Elektra
	Soft Parade	Elektra
	Waiting for the Sun	Elektra
Bob Dylan	Another Side of Bob Dylan	Columbia
	Bob Dylan	Columbia
	Freewheelin' Bob Dylan	Columbia
	Highway 61 Revisited	Columbia
	New Morning	Columbia
	Times They Are A'Changing	Columbia
Richard and Mimi Fariña	Memories	Vanguard
	Reflections in a Crystal Wind	Vanguard
The Fugs	The Belle of Avenue A	Reprise
	The Fugs	Esp
	The Fugs, At Last Live at the Fillmore East	Reprise
	Golden Filth	Reprise
	It Crawled into my Hand, Honest	Reprise
	Tenderness Junction	Reprise
Arlo Guthrie	Alice's Restaurant	Reprise
	Arlo	Reprise
	Running Down The Road	Reprise
	Washington County	Reprise
Janis Ian	For All the Seasons of Your Mind	Verve-Forecast
	Janis Ian	MGM
	The Secret Life of J. Eddy Fink	Verve-Forecast
	Who Really Cares	Verve-Forecast
Jesus Christ Superstar		Decca
Ian and Sylvia	Four Strong Winds	Vanguard
	Full Circle	MGM
	Ian and Sylvia	Vanguard
	Lovin' Sound	MGM
The Incredible String Band	The Big Huge	Elektra
	Changing Horses	Elektra
	5000 Spirits	Elektra
	I Looked Up	Elektra
	Wee Tam	Elektra

Elton John	*Elton John*	Uni
	Tumbleweed Connection	Uni
King Crimson	*In the Wake of Poseidon*	Atco
Gordon Lightfoot	*Back Here on Earth*	United Artists
	Lightfoot	United Artists
	Sit Down Young Stranger	Reprise
	Sunday Concert	United Artists
	Way I Feel	United Artists
Buzz Linhart	*Buzzy*	Philips
Rod McKuen	*The Best of Rod McKuen*	Victor
	Rod McKuen Sings His Own	Victor
	The Sea, The Earth, The Sky	Warner Bros.
	The Single Man	Victor
Melanie	*Born to Be*	Buddah
	Candles in the Rain	Buddah
	The Good Book	Buddah
	Leftover Wine	Buddah
	Melanie	Buddah
Joni Mitchell	*Clouds*	Reprise
	Joni Mitchell	Reprise
	Ladies of the Canyon	Reprise
Van Morrison	*Astral Weeks*	Warner Bros.
	Blowin Your Mind	Bang
	Moondance	Warner Bros.
	Van Morrision (His Band and the Street Choir)	Warner Bros.
Fred Neil	*Bleecker & MacDougal*	Elektra
	Everybody's Talkin'	Capitol
	Fred Neil Sessions	Capitol
Lauro Nyro	*Eli and the Thirteenth Confession*	Columbia
	Laura Nyro: The First Songs	Verve-Forecast
	New York Tendaberry	Columbia
Phil Ochs	*All the News That's Fit to Sing*	Elektra
	Family Portrait	A & M
	I Ain't Marching Anymore	Elektra
	Phil Ochs in Concert	Elektra
	Rehearsals for Retirement	A & M
	Tape from California	A & M

Van Dyke Parks	*Song Cycle*	Warner Bros.
Tom Paxton	*Morning Again*	Elektra
	Newport Broadside	Vanguard
	Outward Bound	Elektra
	Ramblin' Boy	Elektra
Procol Harum	*Home*	A & M
	Salty Dog	A & M
	Shine on Brightly	A & M
Buffy Sainte-Marie	*Fire and Fleet and*	
	Candlelight	Vanguard
	Illuminations	Vanguard
	Many a Mile	Vanguard
Simon and Garfunkel	*Bookends*	Columbia
	Bridge Over Troubled Water	Columbia
	Parsley, Sage, Rosemary	
	and Thyme	Columbia
James Taylor	*James Taylor*	Apple
	James Taylor and the Original	
	Flying Machine	Euphoria
	Sweet Baby James	Warner Bros.
Livingston Taylor	*Livingston Taylor*	Capricorn
Jerry Jeff Walker	*Mr. Bojangles*	Atco
Neil Young	*After the Gold Rush*	Reprise
	Everybody Knows This	
	Is Nowhere	Reprise
	Neil Young	Reprise

Index

The following is an alphabetical guide in three separate lists for authors, song titles and first lines.

FIRST LINES

DATE DUE

GAYLORD   PRINTED IN U.S.A